A Mother's
Adoption Journey

A Mother's Adoption Journey

Darlene Ryan

NATIONAL LIBRARY OF CANADA CATALOGUING IN PUBLICATION DATA

Ryan, Darlene, 1958-
A mother's adoption journey

ISBN 1-896764-49-5

1. Ryan, Darlene, 1958- 2. Adoptive parents — Biography.
3. Adoption — Canada 4. Adoption — United States. I. Title.

HV874.82.R93A3 2001   362.73'4'092   C2001-903012-6

Edited by Sarah Swartz
Designed by Stephanie Martin

Printed and bound in Canada

*Second Story Press gratefully acknowledges the support of the
Ontario Arts Council and the Canada Council for the Arts for our publishing program.
We acknowledge the financial support of the Government of Canada through the
Book Publishing Industry Development Program.*

Published by
Second Story Press
720 Bathurst Street, Suite 301
Toronto, Canada
M5S 2R4

www.secondstorypress.on.ca

For Lauren

TABLE OF CONTENTS

ACKNOWLEDGEMENTS

THIS BOOK began as a journal for my daughter, a chronicle of the process that created our family. There are many people who helped me as this book evolved from that journal. I gratefully acknowledge their assistance, especially that of Margie Wolfe and Sarah Swartz.

As well, many people went out of their way to help us during Lauren's adoption. Chris Campbell and his staff at Mail Boxes Etc copied, faxed, and on occasion stalled the FedEx driver. Andrew Gorham and his crew made our home a safe place for a nosy toddler. Dr. Tom Peters and Dr. Patricia Ramsey provided exemplary medical care. Karen Williamson supplied legal expertise and encouragement.

Special thanks go to Jennifer Dawson and Martha Maslen of The Children's Bridge. Without them our family wouldn't exist. My thanks go also to the families who shared our journey to China.

Heather Fletcher, Rhonda and Robert Brown, Anne and Everett Runtz and Pearl Nixon could always be counted on for support.

Sandi Ford and Janelle Domini have been loving "big sisters" to Lauren.

And my husband, Patrick, has been and is an unwavering source of patience, love and encouragement. I couldn't ask for a better partner or father for our daughter.

Thank you.

PROLOGUE

MY FATHER died when I was two. His mother died when he was five. I didn't connect my father with my reluctance to be a parent or with my sudden consuming desire to have a child after all.

Everything I know about my dad comes from other people. I have his teeth, his impatient streak and his stick-straight hair. And now I have the family he missed out on. Having a family was everything to my father. For him there had been no Christmas, no birthday cakes, no one to kiss banged knees or scare away the bogeyman. His own father was gone, working in the woods for weeks at a time. His grandmother was cold and angry. The only mothering he got was from his sister, just three years older.

My father wanted to give his children, and maybe in a way himself, what he'd never had — two parents and a warm, loving place to come home to. And just when he'd finally done that, he died.

For most of my life I'd doubted my abilities as a parent. I never thought I'd be "good enough." Now I wonder if somewhere inside I was thinking of my dad. After all if this man, who'd taken on hero qualities in my mind, couldn't create a happy ending, how could I?

I was almost thirty-nine years old when I was overwhelmed with longing for a child that wouldn't go away — a feeling that seemed to come out of nowhere. I changed my life. I changed myself. I did things I *knew* I couldn't do to make that happen. My father never had his thirty-ninth birthday. He died two months before.

Now I think maybe it wasn't just my biological clock I suddenly heard. Maybe it was my life's clock taking me past the point where my father's life ended. Maybe it was the part of him that continues in me, giving me a push, whispering, "Do it."

My daughter has two parents who love her. She's secure. She's happy. She has what my dad didn't have. What I didn't have. And I realize that I haven't just created a family for my daughter. I've made one for myself. I finished what my father began.

When my husband and I decided to have a child, I started keeping a journal for the baby. (I've been writing since I figured out letters made words.) I knew however we ended up with a child, it wasn't going to be easy. I was thirty-eight, he was forty-nine when we began. I knew someday our child would have questions, and I wanted to be able to give answers that hadn't gotten too rosy with time.

This book evolved from that journal. I tried to be honest about how I felt and what I did — especially when I didn't come out looking so great. Some adoption memoirs are works of lyrical musing, written by people who never turn the telephone into psychedelic spaghetti, or dance around the living room in their underwear. This isn't that kind of story. I made mistakes. I was obnoxious. I got frustrated. I was wildly happy and lower than I've ever been. And I got the most incredible gift. My daughter. My family.

This is more than the chronicle of an adoption. It's the story of the making of a family.

INTRODUCTION

In the simplest terms, international adoption means adopting a child from a country other than your own. More would-be parents are choosing this route to create their family, because the number of babies available for adoption in Canada is declining. But international adoption often means creating a multicultural and multiracial family, which can be challenging. It brings with it new traditions, new celebrations, new ideas and new insights.

When my husband and I began investigating international adoption, I was looking for facts. What was the process? Which organizations would I need to contact? What would it cost? How long would it take? And, most importantly, was international adoption really something that would work for us? I searched bookstores and the library, but I couldn't find a book with all the practical information that would guide me, step-by-step, through the international adoption process.

As we looked for ideas we kept coming across the name of a particular adoption agency, The Children's Bridge. As foolhardy as it seems now, we put our trust and our hopes for a child in their hands — based solely on our instincts. And on October 4, 1998, I held my daughter for the first time.

During the twenty-two months it took us to get to that moment, I spent more time searching for a book that discussed the emotional and psychological aspects of the adoption process. I had begun keeping a journal when we first started talking about having a child. A lot of my uncertainties and frustration ended up on those pages. I wondered if I was the only one who felt so emotional, so inadequate, so enraged sometimes.

This book is the kind of book I was looking for when I started my journey into motherhood: the facts and the emotions of the adoption process. It is divided into five sections, each representing a different stage of adoption. "Stage One: Making the Decisions" discusses the practical choices that you need to make, either alone or with a partner: to have a child, whether adoption is the best method for you, and whether to go with international adoption. This is the stage at which you may need to think about what creating a family means to you.

"Stage Two: Researching and Planning" deals with the search for more information. Not only will you have to decide from which country you would like to adopt, you will also need to investigate many different adoption agencies in order to choose the one which will work well for you in the months ahead.

Some adoptive parents find "Stage Three: The Waiting Period" the most difficult. During this stage, you must cope with most of the seemingly unending paperwork and bureaucracy both in your country and in the country of your child's birth. You will also be dealing with the agency workers and social workers; you will be interviewed and your home will be visited as part of the "home study." As well as a time for practicing infinite patience, this is also when you will be making preparations for the arrival of your child.

"Stage Four: The Trip Abroad" brings your child into your life. It may also be one of the few opportunities you have to experience life in your child's birthplace. The challenge while you're there is to learn as much as you can, while going through the intense emotions of bonding with your child. You will be creating memories and gathering images for your child to treasure in the future.

The last section of the book, "Stage Five: Life With Your Child," deals with creating a new family once you have your son or daughter. Not only will you need to adjust to the demands of being a parent, but you will also need to deal with the realities of life in a multicultural family both inside and outside your home. As your child grows older, the issues will change, as will your insights.

Each section of the book begins with the information you will need for that stage of the adoption process. Each section also includes my journal entries at that stage. They are a record of my ups and downs, my uncertainties and frustration, and the ultimate joys and challenges I encountered.

Although my experiences and feelings at each stage were unique to me, I hope they will give you encouragement and support as you go through your own journey.

THE INTERNATIONAL ADOPTION PROCESS

The following pages are a brief explanation of the international adoption process. Each part of the process will be explained in depth, with more detail, later in the book.

If you're considering international adoption, you should be aware that the process takes time, money and a lot of patience. There are certain procedures and regulations you need to follow depending on where you live and from which country you want to adopt. Specifics may vary, but the general guidelines will be similar.

As a standard, sixty-six countries, including Canada, drafted The Hague Convention on Intercountry Adoption in May 1993 to better protect children offered for adoption. By August 2000, some thirty-nine, including Canada, had implemented the Convention. The Hague Convention's objectives are to safeguard children by establishing a cooperative relationship between a child's birth country and the adopting country, and to prevent the trafficking, sale, abduction and exploitation of children.

LIVING IN CANADA

In Canada, the regulations on adoption are defined by each province. As well, the country you choose to adopt from will have its own specific requirements and restrictions. The following information is intended as a general guideline only. For the most up-to-date information contact an adoption agency and your province's adoption services office. Requirements such as the minimum or maximum age of the adoptive parents and their marital status vary, depending on the country you would like to adopt from. Some countries allow single persons to adopt; others will not. You may be required to travel to and spend some time in the country. (Contact the provincial public health department's travel clinic or your doctor to arrange for the necessary immunizations.)

Once you have decided on a country, you will need to choose an experienced adoption agency or facilitator. An agency may work with one or several countries. The agency's job is to help you meet all the requirements to complete your adoption. Look for adoption support groups in your area and talk to parents who've adopted internationally for recommendations. Check potential agencies with their local Better Business Bureau to see if there have been any complaints about the agency. Ask the agency for references and check them.

Contact the Department of Family and Community Social Services (also called Family and Youth Services or Ministry of Children and Families depending on the province) to receive their application package, be assigned a social worker and arrange for a home study.

Every adoption requires a home study, paid for by the adoptive parents. The home study is a written report on the prospective parents. It involves a series of interviews and a home visit with a private social worker who has been approved by the province. The final, written report documents that you will be suitable parents and can provide a loving, nurturing home. Once the home study is approved, the province will issue its letter of approval.

Keep in mind that costs for an international adoption, including travel, can top twenty thousand dollars.

DOCUMENTS

You'll need a variety of documents for both the home study and your adoption dossier. You may require any or all of those listed below, depending upon the requirements of your province and of the country from which you are adopting. This is a general list. Your adoption facilitator and your social worker will give you specifics.

- Birth certificates of both prospective parents
- Marriage certificate
- Divorce decree (if applicable)
- Passports
- Criminal background check with fingerprints (contact the Royal Canadian Mounted Police)
- Letters from your employers confirming employment

- Budget/financial statement
- Letter from your bank verifying financial status
- Letter from your family doctor stating both parents are in good physical and mental health
- Names, addresses and phone numbers of at least three references
- Photo of the adoptive parents and an exterior photo of your home

Most countries that have children available for adoption require the documents in the adoption dossier to be notarized. You must also supply several copies. In addition, some countries will require authenticated translations of the documents. Check this with your facilitator. Don't forget to keep extra copies of everything.

IMMIGRATION

Canadian law requires that all immigrants be sponsored, including children adopted in other countries by Canadians. You will need the *Application to Sponsor Family Class Relative*. If your agency doesn't have the application forms you can visit the Web site for Citizenship and Immigration Canada: www.cic.gc.ca.

LIVING IN THE UNITED STATES

Adoption regulations differ somewhat by state. You must also follow Immigration and Naturalization Service rules for immigration. These are intended as general guidelines only. For specifics, work with a reputable, experienced adoption agency. The Office of Children's Issues in the State Department is an excellent source of international adoption information. They can provide you with country-specific adoption information flyers.

Select a licensed adoption agency experienced in working in the country from which you are considering adopting. Check for complaints against the agency with the state Attorney General's office. Find out what services the agency provides. Ask for references and check them thoroughly.

All US adoptions require a home study. This report is completed by an adoption agency social worker or by an independent licensed social worker. State laws or state regulations govern who can provide home study services in each state. The cost of the home study depends on which agency or practitioner is conducting the study. The fee for a home study and parent preparation can range from seven hundred to twenty-five hundred dollars. (Source: the *National Adoption Information Clearinghouse*)

DOCUMENTS

(The following list is reprinted, with permission, from the *National Adoption Information Clearinghouse.*)

You will need to compile a variety of documents for the home study and the document dossier for the foreign court. The required documents usually include, but are not limited to, the following:
- Birth certificates of both prospective adoptive parents
- Marriage license
- A letter from a physician confirming the prospective parents' good health
- Financial statements, including tax returns, statements of assets and liabilities, and letters from your bank describing your accounts
- Letters from your employer confirming position, salary and length of employment
- Letters of recommendation from friends and associates
- Police records
- Child abuse clearance
- Psychological evaluations

IMMIGRATION

The Immigration and Naturalization Service recommends that all prospective adoptive parents file *INS form 1-600A*, the *Application for Advance Processing of Orphan Petition*. After you have been assigned a child you will need to complete *INS form I-600, Petition to Classify Orphan as an Immediate Relative*. For more information, visit the INS Web site or request the information booklet, *The Immigration of Adopted and Prospective Adoptive Children*, from your local INS office.

Note: Amendments to the Immigration and Nationality Act went into effect on February 27, 2001. They provide for automatic citizenship, under certain conditions, for children born abroad. Contact your local INS office for information.

Stage One:
MAKING THE DECISIONS

For most people, the image they hold of their child is that of a healthy baby who looks like them — his hair, her smile, his perfect pitch, her smarts. Adoption means changing that mental picture. For some people it isn't that difficult to make the decision to adopt. They've accepted that they can't have a biological child, or they've decided not to. Adoption is the next step in the process of creating a family. Some even choose adoption for ideological reasons, deciding not to bring children into what they see as an already overcrowded, overstressed world. For them it's more important to use their love and resources to create a family for a child who has already been born.

But for most adoptive parents the decision doesn't come that quickly or that easily. In our society, having a baby usually means having a biological child. And when a couple is infertile, we tend to see them as flawed in some way. We speculate about which partner is infertile, whose fault it is — and sympathize with the other.

"I felt worthless." "It was like I was defective." "I felt like I was only half a person." Those are some of the things an indiviual feels when he or she can't have a biological child, along with anger, grief and a sense that the world is not fair. It takes time to deal with all those feelings.

If the concept of creating a child with someone you love has been important to you, then you need to think and talk about those feelings before you can adjust to a new way of creating a family. Maybe that means hiding out with your partner, talking, grieving. Or perhaps it means reaching out to family and friends. For some, a ritual to say good-bye to the baby that will never be helps. Some choose to write a letter to the child. Others attend religious services in memory of children who have died. Some find peace by burying a symbol, something that has special meaning to them.

In some cases, time makes the decision easier. "[At first] I wouldn't even talk about adoption," a new father confided as we watched our children playing. "We did all the medical stuff and it didn't work. It didn't look like it was ever going to work. But this [adoption] did."

For me, the struggle was deciding which would give me the best chance of having a child soon, biology or adoption. There was no child in my mind I needed to let go. And I was fortunate. Even though I didn't choose to have a biological child, that was still a possibility for me.

To adoptive parents, not having a child is the worst kind of pain. As difficult as it may be to give up the child that lived in their imagination, it's unthinkable to never be parents. "We spent years trying for a baby," one mother shared as we walked up and down the hotel hallway in Beijing with our daughters. "I was numb. The only time I had any hope was when we started talking about adoption."

For some people, easing the anguish of their partner is what makes the decision. "I never wanted to see that look on her face again," one man said about his wife, after a devastating miscarriage.

Single persons struggle with similar issues about adoption as couples. One mother shared how she came to the decision to adopt. "Whenever I had a man in my life, it just didn't work out. One day I realized I was running out of time. It was now or never."

Anyone thinking about adopting without a partner needs a support system — people with whom to share ideas and who will offer encouragement. All parents need a safety net of family and friends. For single parents, that safety net is even more crucial.

Finances are an important part of the decision as well. A single parent must have the resources to pay the costs of adopting (internationally can cost twenty thousand dollars or more), as well as show she can support the new family.

For gays and lesbians who wish to adopt, there's the decision of whether or not to disclose their sexuality. Many choose to keep their sexual orientation private. Others insist it's wrong to hide part of their identity; they feel acceptance and change will only come from honesty.

Some gay adoptive parents argue that married couples don't need to discuss their sex lives as part of the adoption process, so why should gays and lesbians. One woman, part of a committed, lesbian relationship, explained that she adopted as a single mother, because she wanted a child, not a political hassle. "It has nothing to do with whether I will be a good parent." Many adoption facilitators and social workers believe that gays and lesbians can be excellent parents, and if they suspect the person they're working with is gay, they may avoid potential problems by not asking any questions relating to sexual orientation.

It's important to know there are no foreign countries open to adoption that allow gays and lesbians to adopt. Many of these countries consider homosexuality a crime. If discovered, a social worker who lied about an adopting parent's sexual orientation could be out of a job. An agency that knowingly placed a child with a homosexual parent could be put out of business.

CHOOSING BETWEEN DOMESTIC AND INTERNATIONAL ADOPTION

Part of making the decision to adopt is choosing between domestic and international adoption. Domestic adoptions may be public or private. Public adoptions are arranged through the province's adoption services office. The wait for a newborn can be eight years or more. Private adoptions aren't available to everyone. Each province has different regulations covering what type of private adoptions they allow and what procedures must be followed.

However, thousands of special needs children are available in Canada — children who are older, children who have emotional or physical problems, children who have been abused.

But not everyone can be a parent to these children. Not everyone wants to. Many people want to adopt an infant, because a baby is less likely to have been abused and less likely to have severe psychological problems. A child less than a year old will probably have an easier time bonding with adoptive parents. We know that children who haven't formed strong, healthy attachments with parents in their early life can have trouble forming relationships for the rest of their lives.

Some parents may choose a special needs child the second time they adopt, possibly because they have more confidence in their parenting. Choosing to adopt a special needs child means taking a deep look at your strengths, your skills, your biases, your weaknesses. Love heals many things, but not everything.

Some adoptive parents want the experience of raising a baby at least once, which is why so many are choosing international adoption. For political and cultural reasons, countries like China and Korea have thousands of healthy babies who need parents.

Many people who decide on foreign adoption talk about the sense of urgency they feel. After years of fertility treatments, or of being with the wrong person or at the wrong place in their life, they don't feel they have much time to waste. The chance to have a baby without years of waiting seems miraculous to someone who has already been waiting for years.

THE ISSUES

Domestic or international, it's important to look at your attitudes about adoption and race before you start the process. How will you feel about your child being of a different ethnicity than you and other members of your family? How do you feel about knowing little or nothing about your child's birth family? How will you answer your child's questions about her origins or his birth family? If you do feel uncomfortable about any of these issues you need to think about your reasons before you go forward with an interracial or multi-ethnic adoption.

And how will you deal with prejudice outside your home? What will you say to people who ask impertinent questions? With so much at stake, you can't let ignorance pass, even if it is unintentional. What will you do when your child is put down, embarrassed, called names? How will you feel about speaking out? What will you teach your child? You will be your child's role model. If you don't feel confident about your ability to take on that role or to help your child deal with discrimination, there are counselors and courses that can support you and help you make the right decisions.

"I feel so small-minded," a woman wrote at an on-line adoption Web site. "I don't know if I can be a mother to a baby that looks so different from us. I don't think I can stand up to the things people will say."

You feel what you feel. It's not small-minded to admit your doubts. You need to think and talk about your own biases and attitudes before you can deal with other people's. You'll expect your new family to be treated with respect. Start by offering it.

Children in multiracial families should be prepared for stares and teasing from other kids. The entire family must be prepared for crude comments and ridiculous questions, not just about your child's looks and her heritage, but also about being adopted. Ethnically mixed families need to be aware that they will be challenged by people who believe children should not be adopted out of their culture. Families have heard everything from, "How much did she cost?" to "Does he speak English?" to "Do you have any real kids?" Experienced parents say it helps to have a practiced comeback, even if it's just, "that's none of your business," for the adults, and "that's mean," for the kids.

It may help to talk to someone who's living whatever it is that scares you. I haven't met any adoptive parents who aren't willing to talk and to listen. And it might help to know that when you really are someone's parent, somehow you become stronger, braver and better than you were before. "I don't want to be the poster mother for adoption," I exclaimed to my husband on a frustrating day. He smiled and said, "Well, you are."

Did I miss some important life experience because I didn't give birth? I don't think so. I do know I would have missed the most important person in my life without this child.

Journal

November 4, 1996

I DECIDED I wanted a baby during an episode of *Star Trek: The Next Generation.* It was the two-part Borg episode, which I've probably seen ten times because I'm a sucker for Jonathan Frakes. I started imagining what beautiful, manly little babies he'd make. And then I knew, in that moment, that I wanted a child. All the other things came later. At that moment in front of the television my biological clock didn't start ticking. It suddenly went BONG, BONG, BONG.

I don't know how many times I've said I didn't want a child. What I always meant, what I believed, was that I wouldn't be any good at it. And I thought it was important to be good at everything I tried. As a kid, I was told what most kids are: Do your best. But somehow what I heard was do it better than anyone else.

As I got older I found I didn't always have to be perfect. I could see it wasn't making me happy — just crazy. I was lucky to make friends who didn't expect me to always be the best and didn't care when I wasn't. Watching my friends with their kids, I learned excellent parents have doubts and anxieties and sometimes grope for answers too.

I don't think my change of heart really happened all at once. I think over time my courage has been building. I don't think I can stop myself from wanting a child anymore.

I've never really thought I had what it takes to be someone's mother. I don't know if I have enough patience. Am I competent, loving, or selfless enough to do the job well? I like life clean, organized and on schedule — three things kids almost never are. I have an image in my mind of the perfect mother, which, I admit, was shaped partly by way too many episodes of *The Partridge Family* and *The Brady Bunch.*

I'm shaken by the intensity of my feelings, this sudden surge of longing for a child of my own. I feel excited and scared at the same time. My mind is jumping all over the place the way it does when I haven't had enough sleep. I think I need time just to get used to the idea of actually doing this.

I've always liked to get down on the floor and play with everyone else's kids. I like pushing swings, creating Lego buildings that would give a builder heartburn, and listening to little kid tales where the words fall over each other and the story veers off into wild tangents.

"You're great with kids. You should have kids." I have heard this over and over and over. And it seems the possibility has suddenly taken hold — a tiny voice inside me whispering, "I want this."

I know that a good mother is supposed to put her child first. And all I can think about is how much *I* want to do this. I don't even have a child and I've already flunked the first test.

November 6, 1996

For me, a family of my own has always seemed like a three-foot solid chocolate Easter Bunny. It looks wonderful, but what the heck would I actually do with it if I had it? Because I've always questioned whether I'd be any good as a mother.

I can't whip up creative, nutritious snacks on Ritz crackers between the time the school bus stops at the corner and the kids slam the screen door. I can't tell just by a sideways glance which small person has a load in her Huggies. I can't make Jell-O jigglers. I can make poached sole in wine sauce with julienned vegetables, but I can't make Jell-O. Not if you want it to jiggle instead of pour.

Every woman I know with children seems to have some secret manual, like a witch's book of incantations, so she knows things like how to get two kids to share one cookie, what the hell "ants on a log" are and how to make Jell-O that shakes. I've never admitted to anyone that I don't know how to do motherly things. I'm the type that won't even ask for directions if I'm lost.

So I married someone who didn't want to have children either. On the day we went to get our marriage license, Pat and I met on the sidewalk outside Fowler's Jewelry Store. "Are you sure about this?" he said before we went in. "You know it means no children."

"I'm sure," I said. "I'd be a lousy mother."

"No," he had said. "You just think you would."

But I meant the words. I've meant them through twelve years of marriage. So now, how do I tell him I changed my mind?

November 21, 1996

I haven't said anything to Pat yet. I don't know what to say. But a baby is all I think about these days. I edge closer to the idea every day. The longing reaches into everything I do, like a pool of water spreading across the floor. I know I can't spend the rest of my life without a child. Maybe the desire has always been there and, when I was finally brave enough, it woke up. Still, I remember what I agreed to when I married Pat. Once I say I want a baby, once the words are out, I know I have to do it, no matter what. Even if I end up doing it all alone, living in one little room, carrying two bags of returnables and the baby on my back to the redemption center to get money for formula. I have to have a child. But it's overwhelming to face the thought of maybe not being married anymore.

It's painful to imagine my life without Pat in it. He's been part of it for so long. Then, I think about all the years of the rest of my life stretching out ahead of me without a child and that hurts just as much.

Almost every morning this month I've walked up the trail that runs along the old railway bed and tried to come up with a solution that doesn't leave me feeling raw. And I can't find one. This morning I realized that I'm just going to have to say to Pat, "I want a child." Because as much as it would hurt to lose my husband and my present life, I could get over that. But I couldn't get over never having a baby.

I feel as though I'm choosing between my husband and a baby that doesn't even exist. And now I have to tell my husband that I haven't chosen him.

November 23, 1996

We sat at the table finishing breakfast this morning, and I couldn't get the word "baby" out of my mouth. Later, while Pat read the paper, I started cleaning the kitchen cupboards. I have the same relationship with a scrub brush and a bottle of Lysol that a drunk does with a bottle of gin.

Wrapped in tissue paper at the back of one shelf, I found the blown-glass sugar bowl and cream pitcher I'd gotten for Christmas when I was seventeen. I realized how much I wanted to give these treasures of my past to my own child someday, even if he or she were to say, "Mom, they're ugly!" I wanted to have a tea party on the floor with Kool-Aid in the pitcher and animal crackers in the little bowl with a little person. Suddenly I started to cry.

Pat came in, put his arms around my shoulders and said, "Hey, what's wrong?"

"I don't have anyone to give these to," I bawled. "I think we made a mistake." This wasn't how I'd meant to say it, but now I had blurted it out. My nose was running and I had mascara in one eye.

Pat straightened up and in the second or so of silence before he spoke, it felt to me as though the whole world had stopped.

And then he said quietly, "I've been thinking the same thing. What should we do?"

It occurred to me that maybe I'd had a stroke and was hearing the words I wanted to hear, not what he was really saying. But I wasn't. I've seen all the ways Pat has changed in the dozen years we've been married. I just didn't see this coming.

"Really? Really?" I kept repeating. I couldn't seem to make anything else come out of my mouth.

He nodded. "For most of my life I've been spoiled. To Mum and Dad, I was the could-do-no-wrong only child. In some ways I'm still there. I want to stop being so self-absorbed."

He went into the bathroom and came back with a box of tissues for me. I wiped my eyes and my runny nose. "I've realized all I really have is you," he said. "Mum and Dad are old. I want that ongoing emotional connection with someone else. I want someone else to care about and, yeah, someone to care about me."

I nodded. It was hard not to cry. He handed me another tissue. "We spend so much time with the Browns. It's been fun watching the girls grow up. Then the McShefferys came and I was around Geneva. I started thinking about what it would be like to have my own little girl." He smiled.

"There's something special about being daddy to a little girl. I want that kind of bond too."

"I've been too self-absorbed," he said, squatting down and putting his arms around my waist. "I want to change. I want to do this, if you'll give me a chance."

"Yes," I said. I felt the same way I do after a migraine — limp and foggy. Coming together on this felt like a miracle. Maybe I shouldn't have been so surprised though. Whenever we spent time at the Browns', Pat always had time for Jen and Laura. He'd listen to Jen's stories and Laura would climb up in his lap to play. And the first time the McShefferys came to our house, Pat ended up playing hopscotch in the driveway with Geneva. I had one image of him in my mind and I didn't see he had changed.

December 13, 1996

I know we need a lot more information about our choices before we can make any major decisions. Are we going to have a baby or adopt? That's what we need to decide first. I hadn't made any real plans beyond the "I want a baby" decision. I'd been afraid to.

We talk. We plan. I make lists with the pros and cons of both options, lists of where to find more information. I've prowled the bookstores and raided the library for books about babies, about fertility, about adoption. They're piling up next to my side of the bed; *What to Expect While You're Expecting, Operating Instructions, The Parents' A to Z, Giving Away Simone, The Adoption Reader, Good Morning Merry Sunshine.*

I've been through back issues of *Maclean's* and *Chatelaine* looking for articles that might help, and squinted through months of *The Telegraph Journal* and *The Globe and Mail.*

And I keep asking Pat over and over, "Are you sure? You really do want to do this?" Because I still have moments when I feel like Alice being asked by the White Queen to believe impossible things. But Pat's answer is always the same, "Yes."

I'm beginning to feel paralyzed by the books and piles of paper — articles on fertility and pregnancy after forty — and by all the choices. I'll be thirty-nine in a month and a half and Pat will soon be fifty. We can't just pop out a baby in nine months. Biology or adoption? I can't decide. I'm afraid to decide. I feel as though something in my brain has shut down. All I have is highs and lows with nothing left in the middle.

December 17, 1996

One of our friends is going to be a dad again. I didn't even want to be happy for him when I found out. Instead I sat in the dark on the basement stairs and cried, hurt that it had happened so easily for him, jealous that it wasn't me, scared that maybe it would never be me. Pat found me when he came home and wiped my face with his sleeve. "We've talked about it enough," he said. "I'm calling the doctor. It's a start. If it doesn't work, we'll do something else."

"It's going to happen," I said, not quite sure if I was telling him or maybe making a promise to myself.

December 19, 1996

I'm going to be the oldest mother at kindergarten. I know in the rational side of my brain that doesn't matter. I know thirty-nine isn't old. Or forty. And I can't imagine ever having cosmetic surgery. I didn't like having four stitches taken out of my foot.

Still, I stood in the bathroom this morning and pulled back the sides of my face so I could see what I'd look like with a facelift. I looked like someone had pulled a stocking over my face.

I want to be a mother while I can still run across the yard, push a swing, jump rope, hop on one foot, sit in the branches of the birch tree in the backyard. My knees already sound like the Rice Krispie triplets, and I can make a noise with my left shoulder that sounds like I'm deboning a turkey.

December 27, 1996

If we want to make a baby, Pat will have to have his vasectomy reversed. It was done almost twenty years ago. Another life, another person, he says now.

"What changed with you?" I asked last night. I know it must seem as though I don't trust him, but I still need more answers.

He said, "A lot of things. Me mostly. When I was younger I couldn't imagine having a child because I couldn't imagine being responsible for someone else. And I thought I'd have to give up all the things I wanted to do. But over time that changed." He shrugged. "Maybe I grew up. I remember we were talking one day at work and Frank Pleunis said, 'I think people who don't have kids are missing something.' I don't know if he was talking about me, but I started thinking that maybe I *am* missing something. And the responsibility doesn't scare me the way it used to. I guess mostly I just want a family."

"But you were always so sure you didn't," I said.

"I know," he said. "I used to be pretty arrogant. I'm surprised you married me."

I grinned. "Arrogance can be really attractive until you have to live with it every day."

"I'm sorry." He leaned over and squeezed my hand. "As you get older, you begin to see the cracks in that perfect picture of yourself you have in your head. You see you're human. You see your me-first attitude doesn't work. I really do want this, you know."

Our family doctor has referred Pat to a urologist. The urologist says there's about a thirty percent chance of having a baby in the next couple of years if we go with the reversal surgery. If it goes well. And if I'm fertile. And if I can carry a pregnancy. I don't like all these ifs.

I've already decided I can't use a sperm donor. Not for any moral or religious reasons. The whole thing just makes me uncomfortable. For me, it feels like having a baby with a stranger. Most of the men I know are so cavalier about their sperm. The same guy who'll park his car diagonally across two parking spaces doesn't really worry about where he left his sperm. Maybe because they have so much, it's just too big a hassle to keep track.

I'd need to meet the man and see what kind of person he was. I'd want to be able to tell the baby what I thought of his biological father, not just what I'd learned from an information sheet. I guess that's what the problem is for me. I'd always think of the man as the baby's biological father, not just as a sperm donor.

In just over a year I'll be forty. My eggs have been sitting around for a long time. I know it's not the same as leaving a dozen eggs in the refrigerator for forty years, and then bringing them out to make a cheese omelet. But how do I know they're not a bit "off?"

The risk of birth defects terrifies me. I could love a baby who wasn't perfectly okay, mentally or physically, but what happens when I'm too old or too dead? Who would love him and take care of him when I'm not here? What if I have a miscarriage? And what if I can't get pregnant?

I went back to see our doctor. I sat in the office and listened as she quoted me odds on different birth defects and Down's syndrome. She talked about the risk of miscarriage and gestational diabetes. Nothing she said sounded positive, and finally I asked the question I needed to ask: "Do you think we should try to make a baby?"

"That's your decision," she said.

"I know," I said. "But what do you think?" She smiled and shook her head, and I knew I hadn't conned her at all. "It's your decision," she said.

I don't know what to do. Meanwhile, I keep thinking about my eggs shriveling and getting a little older each day.

December 28, 1996

Pat and I keep passing the trying-to-have-a-biological-child versus adopting-a-child decision back and forth. I feel as though I'm playing a game of catch with the rest of my life as the ball. I am beginning to trust that Pat wants to do this too. But I'm not sure he's ready for what trying for a biological child would mean.

"It has to be your choice," he says. "You're the one who'll be pregnant. It's your body."

"You're the one who has to have the reversal surgery," I counter.

"It's not the same thing," he says. "You're going to take more of the risks and, let's face it, you're the mother. It's whatever you want."

Generally I like to tell other people what to do but right now I feel as though I want someone else to decide. But I know I really couldn't live with a choice someone else made for me. I need to make this decision. I just can't figure out what to do because there are so many "what-ifs" bouncing in my head. What if the surgery doesn't work? What if I can't get pregnant? What if I can't carry the baby to term? What if there's something wrong with the baby?

I'm scared. Whenever I think about starting this process, I feel like something is squeezing my head. "If everything goes well…" I've heard that from our doctor and the urologist. I'm certain the gynecologist will say the same thing. But will everything go well? The doctors can't give me any guarantees.

Maybe all this anxiety means something. I don't know. I don't believe in signs and omens, but I wish someone would send me one. A billboard. Skywriting. A burning bush. Still, I know the ultimate decision has to be mine.

December 30, 1996

I woke up at two minutes after three last night from some kind of mixed-up dream about babies, my hair stuck to my neck wet with sweat. I sat in the big chair in the living room with my old plaid robe pulled around my legs. Suddenly I just knew I couldn't say yes to trying to have a baby. I don't need to make another list of pros and cons. I don't need to do any more research. I don't need to talk to the doctor.

I want a child. Not the chance of one at some nebulous date in the future. I know no one can guarantee a baby for me, but I want something better than "If everything goes well…" I feel I don't have enough time to take that chance.

No one even knows if I could get pregnant or stay pregnant. I can't put my life into this "experiment" for years and maybe still end up without a child. Perhaps it's crazy to make the decision based on just my feelings, but I can't think any more. Right now adoption doesn't feel like a second choice; it feels like the right choice.

January 1, 1997

Maybe this new year will bring a child into my life. I'm convinced adoption is the way to do that. I know that family ties that come from blood connections and intertwined strands of DNA are important to some people. But I know there can be just as much love between people who don't have that tie.

I understand the desire to create a child with someone you love, to see your family and yourself continue. But many of the people I've been closest to don't have any biological bond to me. The Allens, for whom my mother kept house, were the only experience of grandparents I had. They praised my report cards, listened to my stories, paid for swimming lessons and years of scribblers and crayons for school. I've known all the Vandenberghes since we lived in part of their house when I was five. To me they'll always be my cousins. They taught me to spit, swear, play poker and ride a two-wheeler.

For me, family is about love, and that I know I can do.

January 3, 1997

We've decided we're not going to adopt here in Canada. The wait for a baby in New Brunswick is between eight and ten years. It's not much different in other provinces. In this province we're not even permitted to advertise, or to contact doctors or school counselors. If we wait for a baby here, I'll be taking "little it" to kindergarten and then shuffling back home with a walker.

I think searching for a baby overseas is the best choice for us. We have the money to do it. (I knew all those years of being frugal were going to pay off.) In countries like Korea and China, there are lots of babies that need families. In Canada, there are fewer children given up for adoption every year. I've read that more and more single people and couples are adopting internationally. It's their best option. For a lot of single persons, it's their only one. I think it's the only workable option for us as well, because I don't want to wait for years. I know that we won't be the same as the other families on our street, but I can learn how to deal with that.

Stage Two
RESEARCH AND PLANNING

If you want to adopt in Canada, either in your own province or another one, the first step in your research is to contact your province's Adoption Services office. You should be able to find the number in the provincial government listings in your phone book.

The rules for both public and private adoptions differ from province to province. For instance, in Quebec at the time of this writing, privately adopting a child born or living in the province is not allowed. In New Brunswick adoptive parents are not permitted to advertise to find a birth mother who may be considering adoption.

If you're pursuing an international adoption, you'll have to decide which country to adopt from and which adoption facilitator to use. Get as much information as you can, from as many different sources as you can find.

I don't recommend what I did. I came across an agency that had been written about several times — always with positive comments. I contacted them and they became our adoption facilitators.

For an international adoption, it's extremely important to research various countries and agencies. The agency I chose was competent, experienced and great to work with. In hindsight I realize it was lucky that something didn't go wrong, because I made my decision based on just a feeling instead of research.

The following suggestions come from my own experience and from the experiences of parents who have already adopted. In turn, you should always do what works best for you.

Be organized. Good research and extensive planning generate more paperwork than you might expect. I used a cardboard file box and a three-ring binder throughout the adoption to keep everything organized. Correspondence went in the binder. Everything else went into labeled nine-by-twelve envelopes in the box. I made a list of things to do every day. (I do that with everything in my life.)

Other people use their computers to keep track of what needs to be done. Some post a master list on the wall. One couple used their spare bedroom as an "adoption office," organizing stacks of documents all over the floor.

If you're part of a couple, you'll need to decide how to divide up the research and the paperwork. In our case, I took care of almost all of it. My husband's job was in another city, two-and-a-half hours away. Since I was working as a freelance writer, I had a lot more flexibility.

RESEARCH THE COUNTRY

Your first step is to find out which countries allow international adoption. Most bookstores will have several recent books about foreign adoption or they'll be able to order them for you. A lot of Web sites are devoted to adoption, and to international adoption in particular. The *Adoption Helper* newsletter and Web site (www.familyhelper.net) are excellent sources of information. So is the Office of Children's Issues, at the US State Department (http://travel.state.gov/int'ladoption.html). Typing "international adoption" into any Internet search engine will give you hundreds of references for more information.

Once you have a list of countries, you'll need to narrow down the choices. Think about the following questions:

Do you fit within the country's requirements?

How old are you? Many countries have age restrictions.

Are you married? Some countries won't permit single persons to adopt.

Have you been divorced? In some countries only one divorce for each parent is acceptable.

Do you have any children? You may not be permitted to adopt from some places if you already have more than a certain number of children.

Do you have a preference for the age or sex of your child? For example, the majority of children available for adoption from China are girls.

What is your ancestry? Did part of your family come from Eastern Europe, South America or Asia? Would you like that link with your child? Or do you have a special interest in another culture?

What's the political situation in the country? If the government is unstable, the adoption process may suddenly get bogged down or be suspended. What reputation does the adoption process have? Are there rumors of corruption or baby selling?

Sometimes the rumors are true. Try to track the source of the story. Is this something you've read on a Web site? E-mail a request for more information. If this is something you came across in a newspaper or magazine, call, write or e-mail the reporter. If someone tells you the story, ask where he or she heard it.

For more information subscribe to the *Adoption Helper* newsletter and visit their Web site. And look for articles in major newspapers such as *The Globe and Mail.* Your library may have back issues on microfilm. *The New York Times* is on-line, with hundreds of articles in its archives.

If you'd like to learn more about some of the countries you're considering, search through recent issues of *National Geographic* magazine. The Lonely Planet guidebooks are also filled with information about the people, history, culture and geography of many countries. Geography books from the children's section of the library are great for getting an overview of a country.

Contact the international adoption support group in your area. To find it, search for adoption support groups on-line. You can also call the multicultural association if there is one where you live, or get in touch with the provincial adoption services office.

Talk to people who've adopted from different countries. Ask about their experiences and any problems they had. If it's possible, meet their children. Can you picture yourself as the parent of a similar child?

RESEARCH THE AGENCY

International adoption is complicated and frustrating. The agency's job is to help you satisfy the requirements of the country you're adopting from. A competent adoption consultant/facilitator will steer you through the process before you leave and when you travel to the country. If the agency is good, staff will hold your hand when you need it (sometimes literally), as well as help you find your sense of humor again. The right facilitator for you will have the experience and knowledge to help you complete your adoption, while reassuring you when you need support. They're one of the most important parts of the process. For me, the competence of the agency was one of the factors that made me decide to adopt from China.

The more information you have before you decide on an agency the better. Visit adoption Web sites. If you're not on-line, most libraries are and have computers you can use and staff to get you started. Read. Talk to parents who've adopted from the country you've chosen. When you don't understand something, ask — even if you think it's a stupid question.

Once you have a list of potential agencies, visit their Web sites and write for their information packages. Ask if the agency will be having an information session in your area. If they're planning one, make sure to go. At every step make lots of notes. There will be way too much information to keep in your head.

By this point, you should be able to shorten your list. You might prefer a smaller agency that works with just a few countries. Maybe you'd like an agency run by people who share your religious or political beliefs. You might be more comfortable with a facilitator in your own province. There may be one or two agencies that seem to be recommended by many people.

Contact each agency on your short list in person or by telephone. You need to learn more about the agency's competence, experience and its "personality." Get the following information:

Ask about the adoption process. Is the agency up-to-date on regulations and time frames? Can they explain what's involved clearly and simply to you?

Has someone from the agency recently visited the country you've chosen? Maintaining personal relationships with adoption personnel in the country is important if there are unexpected problems.

What costs are involved? What is the facilitator's fee?

What services does the agency offer? Are there parts of the process you must handle yourself?

How long has the agency been in business? How many adoptions did the agency handle last year? How many from your country?

Ask for references from parents who have adopted in the last six months and contact them.

Be aware that a reputable agency won't make any specific promises about the sex, age or health of your child. They should be able to give you an age range and tell you, for instance, if it's more likely your child will be a girl. They can speak in general terms about the health of the babies, based on their experience, but they shouldn't offer any certainties.

What kind of impression do you get from the staff member you're talking to? Is this person friendly, pleasant, easy to talk to? Is he or she organized? Can he or she answer your questions? Do you feel comfortable with this staff member? A good match between yourself and the personnel you will be working with is very important.

By now one agency may stand out as the right fit for you. Think about what's important to you. Review the facts.

THE HOME STUDY

Rules for international adoption vary from province to province. Contact your province's Adoption Services office. Depending on the province, you'll be matched with a social worker who will oversee the adoption and make sure you meet all of the province's requirements. You'll be sent an application form and the other paperwork the province requires. Your social worker may also help you arrange the home study, which you must pay for. In some provinces, you must use another, private social worker, approved by the province, for your home study.

A home study must be done for all adoptions, domestic and international. The purpose of the home study isn't just to assure everyone that you'll be a good parent. Its main focus is to help you think about and prepare for all the changes your child will bring to your life.

Your social worker doesn't ask all the questions just to make you crazy. She has guidelines she must follow to satisfy the province and adoption officials in the country you'll be adopting from. She's educated and experienced in adoption. She knows which issues you should be thinking about before you bring your child home.

At this point there are a lot of plans to make. (Write them in pencil. They'll change.) How will you pay for everything? An international adoption can cost more than twenty thousand dollars. Along with the cost of the home study there are fees to be paid for your criminal background check, notarizing and translating documents, immigration and more. Add to your list travel costs and the agency's facilitation fee. If you need help, The National Bank of Canada offers a loan program to finance an international adoption.

If you haven't begun doing so already, the home study will get you thinking about some of the practical things you need to do — like getting your home ready for the baby — as well as how you'll deal with the changes and challenges your child will bring to your life.

The home study really isn't a giant test — even though it feels like that sometimes. It's really the mechanics behind a plan for parenting. How will you teach your religious beliefs? What kind of a support system do you have? What will you say to your child about being adopted? How will you teach her about her heritage? How will you deal with prejudice? All these issues are covered in the home study.

When you feel frustrated and stymied by all the rules and mounds of paperwork, remember not to take it out on your social worker. She didn't set up the system and she doesn't have the power to change it. (Instead, complain to your mother, your partner, your best friend, your teddy bear or the cat next door.) You won't be the only case your social worker has. You want her to take care of you right now, as do all her other clients. Listen to her suggestions. If you run into problems talk them through together. It may or may not be possible to change social workers.

Remember to say "please" and "thank you." It's easy to get so stressed that good manners disappear. As one father put it, "Whenever you have the choice to scream or be nice, be nice."

Journal

January 21, 1997

I'VE WRITTEN to an adoption agency/facilitator, The Children's Bridge. I've come across three different articles about them, all very positive. The Children's Bridge arranges international adoptions from China.

We've already eliminated some countries as possible places to adopt from. For some of them, we're too old, or we're not really considered infertile. Anywhere the political situation is unstable, so are adoptions. The process can suddenly shut down for months.

I know the adoption process is corrupt in some countries. Babies are stolen. Poor women are coerced into selling their children. I can't steal a baby from another woman.

I think China is a good choice for us. They're more accepting of older parents. By law, Chinese families are only allowed to have one child — part of China's population control program. Within Chinese culture it's considered a son's duty to work the family's land, continue the family name and care for his parents. So boys are valued more highly. And there are thousands of baby girls waiting for families. Conditions are good in the orphanages, at least in the ones that handle foreign adoption. It's most likely the baby will have been well taken care of while she waits to be adopted.

Still, it bothers me that I could get my child because of discrimination against women in another country. I've tried to rationalize it by saying women are not valued or treated equally everywhere. But I see the contradiction. All the times I've argued and pushed against discrimination and now it's indirectly going to get me what I want.

But if I give up on adopting from China, what will that change? I've decided I'm going to find an organization that works with women and children in China and give them my support. That makes me feel better.

January 28, 1997

I've been reading through everything I received from the *Adoption Helper* newsletter and I feel more certain about China. They say the average wait is six to nine months once the paperwork is done. And they like old fogies like us; the minimum age to adopt is thirty-five. We're too old for some other countries. I tell Pat that's his fault. He skews our average age.

I'm in rebellion. I'm not doing any more research! No more squinting at microfilm. No more lurking in the stacks at the library. No more reading about the government in Guatemala when I should be writing my radio column.

I know I'm acting like a temperamental child. I know this is not the way to do things, to put all my faith in the first agency and the first country I've come across. It's not like me. Usually I over-research. I don't have the emotional energy to do that this time.

I like everything I've found out about China and everything I've found out about Children's Bridge. There aren't any horror stories about babies being stolen or sold. The adoption program in China is very well organized. The babies are generally healthy. It seems if we just do all the paperwork and keep it together until they match us with a baby, we'll have a daughter. It seems as close to a promise as I'm going to get. Right or wrong, I've set my heart on China.

February 5, 1997

Now that we've decided to do this I feel almost frenzied to make it happen. I carry around a lined yellow pad and make lists every day. Today's has a list of parenting books to find at the library, the date of a back issue of *Consumer Reports* that has an article about baby furniture, a herbal supplement they talked about on the *Today Show* and the name of the wrinkle cream advertised in the commercial break.

I'm reading *The Other Mother* by Carol Schaefer. It's the story of a woman's search for the son she put up for adoption. Later I lay in the dark and thought about the woman who will be my baby's first mother. The worst day of her life will be the best day of mine.

I've started watching for the mailman. There should be a letter from Children's Bridge soon. I think I'm making him nervous.

February 12, 1997

Right after New Year's I wrote to an American law firm that "facilitates" adoptions in the States and will work with Canadians. I've had a letter from them.

Independent adoptions seem to be big business in the US. There's some controversy about using facilitators — paying them to find a baby. Some people feel it's too much like buying a baby. It does make me a little uncomfortable.

The lawyer would advertise on our behalf in the States and take care of the legal details, if the firm found a child for us. If. (Or in other words, write the checks and hope.)

I need more assurance than that. Anyway, I still believe in China. I put the letter in the box of research material I have under my desk.

February 21, 1997

I was drawn to China from the beginning of our search. Some kind of synchronicity seemed to be going on. Sitting in the doctor's waiting room, Pat picked up an issue of *Maclean's* and found a feature story about Chinese adoptions. I pulled a library book from the shelf, and a newspaper clipping about a couple who'd adopted from China fluttered to the floor.

Today there was a letter from The Children's Bridge. I've been lurking by the kitchen door, watching out the peephole. As soon as the mailman drops the letters in the box, I count to ten to give him time to get down the driveway — and then I bolt outside.

I held the envelope in my hand trying to get my fingers to work so I could open it, and I could hear myself taking little squeaky breaths. I read the letter over and over and I still can't get some of the words to form sentences. I think it's the same as when you say a word over and over and over. It just stops making sense. Either that or I have had some kind of seizure and don't realize it. There's only one sentence that matters anyway: *Enclosed please find the forms you require to begin the process.*

I need to read everything they sent again tomorrow. All I know is it really is going to happen.

February 27, 1997

Sometimes I feel as though I have two jobs. One of my writing friends says "freelance writer" is just another way of saying, "starving to death," and sometimes I think she's right. But right now, I'm glad that's what I'm doing. I seem to end up doing adoption stuff in the daytime and then writing and editing at night to get my column and the newsletter done. I'm so lucky I can do that. I stayed up until way past midnight getting the newsletter ready to be mailed this morning; folded all the copies, stuck on all the address labels. I mailed them all after lunch and then came home and worked at my other job: the adoption.

I called Health and Community Services. In this province, Adoption Services is under their jurisdiction. Martha Maslen from Children's Bridge said it was important to get in touch with the province and start the paperwork they require.

I talked to Dorothy Frazier, a social worker, to ask what the province will need and to find out about doing a home study. The adoption seems to hinge on the home study. It's a report by a social worker that basically says we're not running a white slavery ring out of our basement or mistreating small farm animals. In New Brunswick, a home study is done by a private practitioner, licensed by the province, not by a social worker employed by Health and Community Services. There are only two social workers licensed to do home studies in our area. And there's a waiting list. It's going to take months.

I tried not to scream. I didn't smash the phone across the room so all the wires were hanging out like psychedelic spaghetti. I did eat half a carton of chocolate chocolate-chip, but I'd have done that anyway.

Dorothy ran down the list of requirements to complete the adoption. We have to have medicals and background checks, provide references, fingerprints. So now I'm a criminal because I want a child? It's just to protect the babies, I keep telling myself. (I like to think that if I was a criminal I'd be smart enough not to get caught, but probably real criminals think that way too.)

I'm doing this regardless of the obstacles. They can take my finger-prints, my picture, I'll even pee in a bottle. I'll stand on my head and sing *O Canada* if that's what I have to do. In fact, I'll sing it standing on my head and peeing in a bottle as they take my fingerprints and my picture if that's what it takes.

I hope it doesn't.

March 3, 1997

I mailed the application forms back to Children's Bridge today. Pat signed everything last night after he came home from Moncton. I'm handling all the paperwork, rather than Pat. I'm here all the time and I can arrange to be free in the daytime. Pat now works as a controller at the area radar control center in Moncton for five days out of nine, so it's harder for him to put time aside for filling out paperwork and chasing down documents. I can write at two in the morning in my bathrobe and sweat socks if I need to. He's been working in Moncton since the control tower closed in Fredericton.

"You sure about this adoption?" I said as I handed Pat the papers. I needed to ask just one last time. He signed first, then set down the pen.

"Yeah, I'm sure," he said. "I'd do this just because I can see how much you want it. But I'm not doing it for that reason. When the tower closed, suddenly I knew I didn't have control of my life. It wasn't my choice and I didn't like it. Working in Moncton isn't the same as controlling in a tower. Suddenly I was in a situation that wasn't easy, doing something I wasn't so good at. I made a lot of mistakes and when you do that, you have to look inside yourself and see what you're lacking. The changes didn't come natu-rally, but I made them and I'm glad. And I'm happy we're doing this."

The adoption is probably going to cost about eighteen thousand dol-lars. Thank goodness we have the money. People who don't have to borrow it — from their parents or the bank — and then worry about paying it back. I'm glad that's one thing I don't have to figure out.

March 13, 1997

We went to Oromocto and had our fingerprints taken at the new RCMP building. It's part of the criminal clearance we need for the province and for

China, to show we're not criminals or child molesters. While we waited in the lobby, I peered into all the light fixtures looking for the security cameras. I didn't find any.

Everything I knew about fingerprinting came from old movies, and the information was wrong. I used to watch a lot of old movies on TV when my mother was working. There's an entire segment of my brain filled with incorrect information.

They use something that looks like a piece of carbon paper, not an inkpad. Each finger is rolled from the left to the right. The officer who did the prints folded my fingers down against my palm and held them so I couldn't mix up the order. At the end, she held all four fingers together and printed them and added the thumb as a double-check. By now those prints are probably in a computer somewhere. There goes my second career as a cat burglar.

March 15, 1997

We've decided to have the bathroom renovated. The tub takes a good fifteen minutes to drain after a bath. I figure there's a hairball in the drainpipe that's been growing for about forty years. The flush mechanism in the toilet breaks about every six weeks. I keep the spare chain in the hall closet, although dental floss will do if it's after nine on a Sunday night.

I'm not sure if this urge to do things is some variation of a pregnant woman's nesting instinct or if it's my mind's way of keeping me occupied, so I don't end up walking back and forth across the bridge holding a sign that says, *Baby Wanted.*

March 29, 1997

Today is Pat's birthday. Fifty. Anne and Ev Runtz are here. They're his big surprise. Not exactly a stripper jumping out of a cake, but close. I miss them since they moved to Cornwall. Ev and I have the same sense of humor. Some people don't think that's a good thing.

Bob and Rhonda Brown are hiding them at their house. We're supposed to just be going down there for dinner. When Anne and Ev were still here, all six of us used to hang out together. I can't wait to tell them about the baby.

April 1, 1997

We got to Bob and Rhonda's and they had hidden Anne and Ev downstairs in the family room. Pat walked in and then froze with his mouth open. "Oh God, Anne and Ev," he said. And then we were all laughing and talking at the same time and I was bouncing around like a big Irish setter. I was happy because Pat was happy and because Anne and Ev were there.

When we told them about the baby, they both got big goofy grins and hugged me. Ev whispered, "You'll be a great mama." No one has said, "Are you out of your mind?" so far, although I keep expecting it to happen. The friends who know us best have been nothing but happy and supportive. If they're thinking, *what the hell are they doing?* they're keeping it in until they're in the car on the way home.

I hope the baby doesn't feel that we did the wrong thing by adopting her. I worry about that. Okay, so I worry about everything. I said to Pat, "What if she hates me? What if she wishes I wasn't her mother? What if she hates that we brought her here?" He just looked at me and said, "What if she loves you?"

The RCMP called this morning. I was trying to sound polite and non-criminal and at the same time think of anything I might have done that would mean I couldn't pass the background check. Turns out I didn't send the correct fee.

April 9, 1997

Today I bought one of my favorite books for the baby, *A Bear Called Paddington.* I loved all the Paddington books and I hope the baby does. Paddington is kind of adopted too.

I want to do everything right. I stood in the grocery store a few days ago reading the labels on all the little jars and boxes of baby food, and I think it would be better if I just made all the baby's food. Except I don't know what kind of chemicals are on all the fruits and vegetables at the store. I'm definitely going to need organic vegetables.

How am I going to do this? I don't know where to buy organic vegetables. And how do I know for sure they haven't been sprayed with something that will make the baby's teeth turn black and keep her from growing over four feet high?

I'm doing the Arts Report on CBC Stereo for a few weeks. I'll know about a lot of the cultural events happening in the province. There has to be some way to use that to impress the social worker when our home study starts.

We passed the Interpol/fingerprint check. I was so relieved my knees went rubbery when I opened the envelope. Even though I knew there was no reason we wouldn't come out clean, I've been inventing scenarios that involve civil disobedience and hiding out in Mexico.

April 15, 1997

I had a letter today from Health and Community Services about going to one of their adoption information sessions. We did that ages ago. I remember that I came home overwhelmed and discouraged because I'd learned the wait for an infant here can be eight or more years and the rules governing private adoption seemed so strict. No advertising. No using doctors or counselors as a way of reaching a woman who might be considering adoption. For a moment I thought I would take to my bed like the heroine of some antebellum novel.

I talked to our social worker, Dorothy Frazier, and got it all straightened out, but then she began telling me about potential problems with international adoptions. It seems there's a lot of debate about whether it's a good idea to adopt a child out of her race and culture. Those opposed say the children lose their ethnic identity and aren't prepared to handle all the discrimination they'll face.

I know we'll be taking the baby away from her culture, but how culturally enriching is life in an orphanage? She will learn about China. It's not as though I'm going to tell her we found her in the cabbage patch. I want her to learn about her background and be proud of it. Chinese traditions and celebrations are going to be part of our lives. And we can teach her how to deal with ignorance.

I would never buy a baby or steal a child from her mother. But if that mother isn't able to look after her baby, it's not wrong for me to be her mother as well.

April 21, 1997

Progress. Dorothy found a social worker in Saint John to do our home study. Saint John is just over an hour away, especially if I'm driving. I told her we were willing to go to Saint John or Moncton. I didn't want to wait months for one of the two social workers who can do home studies here in Fredericton to be available. The home study should start in about a month.

Just the thought of the home study intimidates me. I know that in part it's done to assure the province and China that we have the potential to be good parents. And I know we do, so that's not a problem. I know as well, the point of the home study is to help us think and plan. Are we ready for any health or behavioral problems the baby might have? Do we have a support system, people to help out, give us a break? What will we tell the baby about China? How will we deal with prejudice? I'm sure the social worker will ask those questions and we're ready. Pat and I have already talked about most of this.

And I still feel uncertain. I feel as though I'm crossing a wide rushing brook, stepping from one lichen-covered rock to the next. I'm always one slippery step from falling in.

The contractor and crew arrived this morning to start on the bathroom. One of the first things they did was take apart the old chimney that runs up through the bathroom. When they got just below the floor line, Andrew (the boss) pulled out the liner and a mushroom cloud of soot erupted from the hole. There is a gray layer of soot on everything and sooty footprints all through the house.

I scrubbed the kitchen and all the floors. The rest is going to have to wait until tomorrow. Then I walked over to my mother's apartment for a bath, because my tub is in two pieces on Andrew's truck somewhere.

April 30, 1997

It occurs to me that adoption is in some ways like renovating. It always takes longer than you planned. Just because you have an opinion doesn't mean anyone will pay attention to it. Crying will not work. And you have to figure out how you're going to handle the shit.

The forms have arrived from Health and Community Services. I think it would be easier to just flip open the top of my head and let them pull out all the things they want to know. It strikes me that I could be some kind of a weirdo and how would they ever know? I used to write commercials. I know how to make things sound good. I know what they want to hear. It's not as though I'm stupid enough to give the wrong answers.

So far we have filled out passport applications and fingerprint requests, and gotten our medicals. Now we have more medical forms, another set of criminal record checks, something called the Tressler-Lutheran Service Questionnaire (the touchy-feely forms) and applications that basically want our whole lives on several pieces of paper. The Browns and the Runtzes are going to be our references. I can trust them to make us sound good.

At the bottom of the page, Dorothy had written, "the private practitioner may ask you to prepare an autobiography. This will aid her/him in determining what things in your life have impacted on you to make you the person you are today." Creative writing time.

May 14, 1997

The social worker called from Saint John and I have my first meeting with her on Monday. It should last a couple of hours. I hope I didn't sound as brain-dead on the phone as I feel. I'm alternating between exhilaration and terror. What if she hates me? What if she flunks us?

Her name is Judy Urquhart and she was very nice on the telephone. I really hope I sounded like a rational, functional human being. I have no idea what I said.

This afternoon I thought, *who in their right mind would give me a baby?* Then it occurred to me that anyone who could come up with this inane mountain of paperwork couldn't be in his or her right mind anyway.

The other day I was on my way to the copy shop with my heap of papers and I met a woman I used to work with. When I told her what I was going through she said, "I know how you feel." And I thought, *No you don't. When you wanted a baby you just had sex.*

May 18, 1997

I have a jazzy little red rental car to drive to Saint John, because Pat is in

Moncton working. He left me his cell phone in case I have any problems. The drive should only take about an hour-and-a-quarter, but I'm going to give myself lots of time. I don't want to be late and make a bad first impression.

I have copies of everything I can think of that the social worker might want. Birth certificates, our marriage certificate, last year's tax forms, bankbooks, credit card statements, even a picture of the house. I have stuff she's never even going to think of wanting.

I keep asking myself, how bad can this be? More importantly, how badly can I screw this up? We're just going to talk. I can always talk. It's just about my best skill.

All day I have been saying, *it's going to be okay.* Over and over.

May 19, 1997

I got dressed this morning and spent ten minutes staring in the mirror trying to decide if the lace on my bra showed through my blouse. One of the carpenters showed up with the trim for the new closet in the bathroom. I yanked open the door, threw open my arms and said, "Do you like this blouse?"

"It's very nice," he said. He looked confused, like maybe he'd shown up at the wrong house.

I ran back down the hall, peeled off the shirt and pulled on my second choice. He was still standing in the kitchen doorway. "Do you like this one?" I asked.

"Umm, it's nice too?" he said, as though he wasn't sure what the right answer was. (How can a guy who spent half a day getting three shelves "just right" not be able to tell which blouse looks better?)

Now I can't believe I did something like that. I know what I wear doesn't matter to the social worker. Normally it doesn't matter to me. My style is thrift-store chic. When I get stressed, insignificant things suddenly seem to be so important. I should have called Heather this morning. She's become the friend I talk to the most when I'm crazy. I'm mortified thinking about facing the poor carpenter tomorrow.

I drove fairly fast and got to Saint John early, which was good because

I had time for two nervous pees in Tim Hortons at Simm's Corner.

The social worker, Judy Urquhart, was nothing like what I'd anticipated. I was expecting a cross between She-Who-Must-Be-Obeyed and Gladys with the purse and the hairnet from *Laugh-In*. Judy was like her voice: a bit older than I am, friendly, gentle.

And all we did was talk about me: how I grew up, what it was like to lose my dad when I was so little. I told her about the time I split my toe almost in half and my mother wrapped it in gauze, taped it with masking tape and sent me back out to play. I told her about selling Christmas cards, picking raspberries and walking old Mrs. Stephenson's dog so I could buy my mum a set of pots for Christmas. Flaming orange pots. (She's still using them.) I told her how my sister accidentally stabbed me with a pair of sewing scissors, which I am still convinced is the reason I have no boobs.

Judy listened and wrote.

Talking about my own childhood started me thinking about the kind of childhood I'd like the baby to have. I want her to have the time and the freedom to explore and imagine. And I definitely want her to have the experience of working and saving for some of the things she wants.

I came out of the building with that last-day-of-school feeling — happy, tired and silly — and drove home high on endorphins. Now I feel exhausted, as though I'd run to Saint John and back.

I have homework. Resumes, references, a budget and financial statement and letters from the bank confirming it all. And a list of questions to answer: *Why China? How will we tell the baby she's adopted? How will we teach her about her culture? What kind of support system do we have?*

What does any of this have to do with being a good parent? It's crossed my mind that maybe I should have made a baby in the back of Donnie Driscoll's Toyota when I was a teenager and I had the chance.

May 25, 1997

At least Pat will be with me for the rest of the trips to Saint John. Judy wants to meet with both of us from now on. Pat was there today when Judy and I talked about my "past relationships." I don't have that many. At first I thought it was a good thing. I wouldn't seem promiscuous. I'd seem committed and good mother material. But then I thought, maybe it's a bad thing. Maybe it makes me look anti-social and not good mother material.

I can't believe I'm making such a fundamental change in my life with so much anxiety and so many questions that don't have answers. I just feel it's now or never. And I choose now.

May 31, 1997

The home study should be finished by the end of June. This is very good because I feel on the edge of hysterics from the moment I wake up on the day we have to meet Judy, until we walk into the building. I feel as though I should be breathing into a paper bag. The home study feels like a huge obstacle. If it weren't important, why would they be making us do it?

I can't eat or sleep much before we go. Most of the pressure I feel comes from my own head. I know the home study isn't important in the pass-or-fail sense. It's really just to make sure we've thought everything through. But I still feel that if I make a mistake now, do the wrong thing, say the wrong thing, I will never have a child. It doesn't matter that the rational part of my brain knows this isn't true; the crazy part has a louder voice.

Today all I had to do was listen as Pat told Judy about his childhood and started on his relationships. Of which there are many. I know this because I'm always getting introduced to some woman he knew in university. Always a woman. Never a man.

I read somewhere that the adoption process is like being on a roller coaster — all ups and downs. But I think it's like being on a bus at night. I'm thinking about one of those long-distance buses that stop at every tiny town between two big cities. That's what this whole process is like for me — a lot of stops and starts with long stretches of time when I can't tell if I'm getting anywhere.

I have never wanted to do anything as much as I want to do this. If someone came and built a brick wall at the bottom of the driveway, and it went as far up as I could see, and as far to the left and as far to the right, I would go around it, I would climb over it, I would dig under it, or I would take it down one brick at a time. But it would not stop me from having a child.

June 11, 1997

I think my mother has told everyone she knows that there's a baby coming, even people she barely knows. "The babe," she calls her.

My mother has always kept quiet about me not having children, but she couldn't keep quiet over this. "You're getting older and wiser," she said when we told her.

She hasn't questioned the changes or the reasons; she's too busy being happy. "You know if you'd done this sooner, you'd be going back for a second one," she said.

"Don't get greedy," I told her.

Meanwhile I'm working on our dossier for China.

Here is what they require:

- A letter of application. (Written from the husband's point of view.)
- Photos of us and our house. (We look normal.)
- Letter from our employers. (We're clean, keen and co-operative.)
- Letter from the bank. (We have money.)
- Copies of our birth and marriage certificates.
- Copy of the photo page from our passports.
- Copy of our Interpol clearance. (We're not international criminal masterminds.)
- Letter from our doctor.
- Copy of the home study.
- Copy of our recommendation from Health and Community Services.

And all of it in quintuplicate.

I have always thought of myself as a non-violent person, but today, trying to get all this paper ready, I had the urge to tear a pillow apart with my teeth. I don't think this is something I should share with Judy.

June 13, 1997

Today we told Judy about each other, which was easy. I told her that Pat was kind, patient, even-tempered and that he never gets mad because I won't ask for directions or read instructions. If I had to name someone who didn't like him, I wouldn't be able to. He gets along with everyone while I'm usually gritting my teeth and pretending to smile.

Pat said I was resourceful, funny, motivated and out-going, and that I could handle any disaster. I wanted to say, "No, I just fake it well," but I knew better than to give myself away.

Then we talked about how we plan to raise the baby. I kept wondering if I was giving the "right" answers. I want to be home with her. I want to change diapers and give her bottles and rock her when she cries. I want to sing silly songs and play pat-a-cake and show her off in the stroller. And maybe eventually it will all seem mind-numbingly dull — but I don't think so. Some days it feels as though I've been waiting for this for just a little less than forever.

Judy asked if I thought it would bother me that the baby is adopted. Would I feel I lost something because I hadn't given birth to her? I said, "I won't love our child as if she were mine, I'll love her *because* she is mine. I don't need to see my eyes or my husband's smile in her to think of her as my daughter. I'm eager to discover the person she'll be."

I'll be happier when this part is over. I wish I could explain why this home study has been so hard for me. It feels as though this is the place where I have to be perfect. Even though I know that's not what the home study is for. And it doesn't matter that the rational part of my brain — what little there is still working — knows that.

Mostly, I just have trouble acting normal when I'm nervous.

June 20, 1997

Tonight we went to visit John and Diane McAdam. They adopted a baby from China last year through Children's Bridge. That's who put us in touch with them.

Their daughter, Sydney, is enchanting. She's about a year-and-a-half old. She sat next to me on the floor and "showed" me pictures from China in their photo album, while John and Diane talked about the trip. I actually had a moment when I wondered if I could get Pat to create some kind of diversion and I could scoop up Sydney and run out to the car. Which was silly. Pat is no good at that kind of thing.

It was so good to talk to people who have done this, who understand the process, the problems, the feelings. Everyone I know has been so supportive, but none of them have adopted themselves. Sometimes I feel as though I have to translate everything, almost as though I'm speaking another language, so they can understand what we're going through. It wasn't like that with John and Diane. We speak the same language.

John and Diane went to China with several other families from this area. They get together regularly and they invited us to join them. I'm so glad they did. When the baby gets here it will give her the opportunity to be with families that are just like hers.

Diane gave me tips on what clothes to take to China when we go — squishable and washable. She said absolutely take an umbrella stroller. John showed us what they took for luggage and what kind of electrical adaptor and hotpot they used. As soon as we got home, I made notes in the margin of my list for tomorrow, before everything fell out of my head and got lost.

One thing I learned from John is that I'm never going to be able to cross the street in China. A population of 1.2 billion people makes a lot of traffic. I'm just going to have to grab some Chinese person, close my eyes and go.

June 21, 1997

We're finished with the interview part of the home study. We talked about what problems could potentially arise. Judy asked whether we were afraid of having a child we know so little about.

"What would we really know about her if I'd given birth to her?" I answered. "How could we know what tangle of DNA she'd end up with?" There are things I wouldn't want a child to get from me: my temper, my hair. I think a person is shaped more by the way she's raised. I'd like to know more, so I could tell the baby more about her background. But what I don't know doesn't bother me.

"How will you deal with racism?" Judy wanted to know.

I told Judy that I think racism comes out of ignorance and fear of things and people that are different from what we know. I can teach the baby that. I can teach her it's wrong and it's unfair. I can teach her how to answer back. I can show her that differences can be wonderful. I can show her, always, how loved and special she is.

Pat and I have talked a lot about this. He said he's done a lot of thinking about his own biases and prejudices. He's tried to see where they've come from and he's working on changing his attitudes. "I want to be a good example for her," he said. So do I.

I understand that the baby probably won't bond to us at first. Depending on how old she is, she might not even like us. I know she'll be small and behind in her development. It was hard for me not to say to Judy, "I don't care." I care that the baby is happy, healthy and feels loved, but I don't care what kind of problems she brings with her. I just want her here.

June 22, 1997

I started doing some reading about China. I just want to know a little more about the country and the people. The librarian at the reference desk of the downtown library was really helpful. He found me a book that's a general guide to China with lots of wonderful pictures. And he recommended I try to buy a travel guide to China. I also have a book about the history of Chinese people that's fascinating. The majority of the population is Han Chinese. The rest are different ethnic minorities: Uighurs, Yi, Mongols, Tibetans, Zhuang and several dozen others. The country's history goes back five thousand years. There's so much to learn.

Judy is coming on Tuesday to see our house and the neighborhood. This is the final step in our home study. If I can keep from acting weird for about one more hour, I'll have made it through the home study.

June 23, 1997

It started when we got home from Saint John Saturday night. I walked around the house and it was like I'd put on a pair of those x-ray vision glasses that were advertised on the back of comic books when I was a kid. But instead of seeing the bones in my left hand, all I could see were things that needed to be cleaned. Of course Pat wouldn't take it seriously because it's always been a big joke for everyone who knows me that I'm a bit of a clean freak.

I've vacuumed everything. I pulled out all the furniture. I cleaned all the light fixtures and the heating vents and underneath all the cushions on the couch. I scrubbed the kitchen floor and the bathroom — hands and knees with a scrub brush.

I've almost finished painting the side steps. The deck and the treads need a second coat, but I should be able to do that in the morning. I also mowed the lawn and did all the clipping. Plus I washed the walls in the hall. I think I'm starting to get stoned on Mr. Clean.

June 24, 1997

I've never been so out on the edge in my life. Judy has been and gone. I was showing her around and I could hear my voice getting higher, and I realized I'd said three sentences without taking a breath. She thought the house and the yard looked good, even the big bare spot in the back that doesn't have any topsoil or grass.

After she'd looked at everything, we sat at the table and talked about the neighborhood. I told her about both parks and the walking trail. We can walk to the library and the YMCA. We're close to all three grandparents.

It was a beautiful evening, sunny, but not too warm. Everyone's lawn was mowed, and Pearl's planters were filled with pink geraniums next door. The street sweeper had even looped through early in the afternoon.

I thought with this step done I'd be able to relax. But I still feel as though there is a stack of concrete blocks on my head. Now we wait to read the finished report. As long as she says, "Give them the baby," I don't care what else she writes.

Okay, so I do care, but not very much.

June 25, 1997

I called Dorothy Frazier because Judy had asked me to relay a message. Dorothy told me that when the home study is officially approved, the province will send a "Letter of No Objection" to Immigration. The letter is just what it sounds like: The province has no objection to our adoption. At that point, we may need to have chosen the baby's name. This is not good. We've been putting combinations together and have a "name of the day." I like the name Grace. Pat says it's an old woman's name. At this rate the baby's first name is going to be *Hey* and her middle name will be *You*.

So, I bought a baby name book. I snuck into the Owl's Nest bookstore and jammed it at the bottom of my backpack as soon I'd paid, as though it were porn. I've already discovered names I didn't even know existed.

I didn't know naming a person could be so complicated. We decided no names that can be turned into stupid nicknames. Plus we're not naming the baby after anyone. All the left-out people would get hurt. And no names that are of old girlfriends. (Pat laughed, but I'm not kidding.)

Now that we've told everyone what we're doing, I've noticed some people dropping test sentences in the conversation to find out why we're adopting. "Because we want a child" doesn't seem to be a good enough answer for some of them.

Someone who knew Pat is older than I am asked if he had any grown children. I said, "Not that we know of." No one has asked if I have any grown children. (I like to go with the fantasy that I look too young.)

I've been asked which gynecologist I went to and if we "had" to go to Moncton. There's a fertility clinic at the Georges Dumont Hospital there. One woman I only know slightly, who heard the news from someone else, asked if I'd had a miscarriage. People seem to want to know who's "broken," as though we'd choose adoption because one of us can't be fixed.

I was getting really crazy today, so I called Heather and raved for a while. I don't know what I'd do without her to talk to. She's been an incredible friend. When I told her we were doing this her first words were, "If you need to talk, call me." (I bet she's regretting that.)

I've called late at night when she's been tired. I've called when I know she must have had a long, frustrating day. She never hangs up or tells me to stop whining. She always listens. And I always feel better.

July 6, 1997

My mother came back from Nova Scotia with a teddy bear quilt for the baby. She's wanted to buy baby things from the moment we told her we were going to adopt. "I was meant to have a bunch of grandchildren," she said. Now she has her eye on a high chair for her apartment. I think it looks like something off the bridge of the Starship Enterprise.

I'm glad I'm going to be home with the baby. I want the fun of raising her and I want the crappy stuff too. We can afford to do this. I can work when the baby sleeps. I can get up early or stay up late. Pat gets four days off in a row, so he'll be able to spend a lot of time with her too.

I have lots of backup — Rhonda, Heather, Pearl next door. "You are going to share her with us, aren't you?" Heather asked.

"Yes," I said.

My friend Anne in Cornwall says she's going to do the baby's hair. She says I only know how to do one hairstyle. Mine.

I'm glad the baby will have all three grandparents close by. I didn't have any grandparents and I was jealous of my friends who did. Grandparents love you, spoil you like crazy, bend the rules and tell you embarrassing stories about your parents when they were kids. They let you eat cake for breakfast and read the same story six times in a row. I want the baby to have all that.

Little No-Name has her first teddy bear. Jennifer Brown made it. We've asked the Browns to be the baby's backup family. If something happened to Pat and me I know she'd be safe and loved with them.

Rhonda Brown is a great mother. I know that she would love the baby and protect her and do all the things I want for my daughter if I couldn't. Her daughters, Jen and Laura, are my favorite kids in the whole world.

July 17, 1997

We've been looking for another house or somewhere to build for a long time. I'd like a bigger yard — more privacy, more trees, a garage, a big eat-in kitchen (instead of a table in one corner of the living room), and most of all, a sun porch.

The problem is our target area is very, very small because we're very, very picky. Actually I'm very picky and Pat doesn't care. I don't want to be more than forty minutes on foot from all my haunts, like the library, the bookstores, the thrift shop. Most of the time, I'd rather walk than drive, which is good, because most of the time the car is in Moncton.

Last week I discovered a lot for sale just at the crest of the hill on Golf Club Road. I know the timing is lousy since we're in the middle of the adoption and Pat's away for work more than half the time. But we bought it. For once I didn't think things to death. It's occurred to me that on some level I might be trying to change everything from my old, no-child life. And that this might be a mistake. I keep telling myself if it's a mistake, so what? It's not as though we bought an elephant.

July 18, 1997

The baby has a name. Serena Claire.

Stage Three:
THE WAIT

No matter how long you're told the wait will be, double it and add half an hour. No matter how prepared you are there will be setbacks you didn't anticipate and no one warned you about because "that's never happened before." Regulations and requirements can and will change in the middle of the process. Documents get lost. Social workers get the flu, wreck their cars and have too much work to do. Those are the lessons I learned from waiting to get my daughter.

At this writing the wait from the time the adoption file is sent to the country until the time you'll receive an offer for a child is two to three months for Korea and almost a year for China.

Every step in an adoption is stressful. Some people are overwhelmed by the home study. I was. Others get frazzled trying to gather all the documentation. Before you start, think about ways to cope with the stress. I cleaned my house every time I felt crazy. One father I know went running. Another mother said she "walked miles." Others shot hoops, biked, went swimming, painted the house, dug dandelions out of the lawn.

It helps to have both a physical outlet and an emotional one. Someone close, other than a partner, who will listen while you rant and cry can help get you through any setback. Don't forget to share your good news too.

There's nothing wrong with occasionally eating an entire container of chocolate chocolate-chip ice cream to get through your frustrations, but remember, you do want to be healthy when you go to get your child.

RELATIONSHIPS

In the beginning, when I felt very shaky and uncertain, we only told our parents and our very closest friends. I didn't want to talk a lot, or God forbid, have to explain if the adoption fell through. The people we did tell understood or, if they didn't, at least cared enough not to stay offended.

Later, when it seemed there was less that could go wrong, we told everyone. Then, talking about the baby reassured me that it was really going to happen. There's no question that it helps to have lots of support while you're going through the adoption process, especially during the long stretches where nothing seems to be happening. You need someone to talk to, someone who will sympathize with you, someone to occasionally race to the copy shop and run out for pizza.

Many adoptive parents find they get closer to their own parents. The closer I got to becoming someone's mother, the more amazed I was at how my own mother had managed to raise two children on her own after my father died.

Friends who have children are great sources of advice. They're also great sources for baby furniture, clothes and toys. Many of these friendships become even stronger once you have your child.

Friends without kids are wonderful for reminding you that you're more than just an expectant parent. They're great for cheering you up and dragging you out for some fun whenever you get overloaded — during the adoption and after.

Other adoptive parents are wonderful to talk to. They understand completely what you're going through and they can offer more than just a soft shoulder; they usually have practical suggestions to get by most problems. If you join an international adoption group, when your child arrives she will have the opportunity to be with other families just like her own.

Be aware that everyone in your life might not be as happy as you are about adopting a child. Some single parents find their parents disapprove of raising a child outside marriage. Gay and lesbian parents may discover their families have reservations about gay people as parents. Brothers and sisters who've produced the only grandchildren to this point may feel a bit jealous. Some of your friends may resent your focus on finding a child and the large amount of time it takes up. In the short term, until your child arrives, you might decide to challenge these people on their attitude or just spend less time with them. A lot of the negative attitudes disappear once there's a new little person to love.

Waiting (And Waiting)

After the rush of completing paperwork and doing the home study, the wait to be referred a child seems to stretch out without an end, even if you're lucky and it's just a month or two. It can take as long as a year. But there are advantages to the waiting, even though they probably won't seem like advantages at the time. This is the time to put many of your plans into action. Prepare your home for your child. Prepare yourself physically and mentally, as much as you can, for the trip to get your child and for becoming a parent. Think of this stage as your "pregnancy."

You'll probably find your feelings wavering about everything from the baby's name to what kind of diapers to buy. You can and will change your mind about the small things. Don't worry about this; what really matters is getting your child.

Some adoptive parents take on new projects while they wait. That can be a good idea, if you're doing it for the right reasons and if you can handle the extra stress. We decided to build a house for a lot of wrong reasons. I still wasn't sure I was "good enough" to be a mother, but I knew I could create a house that was good enough and that's what I tried to do. We stopped the project when we realized it wasn't the right decision. Not at this stage.

Many of the following suggestions come out of my own mistakes, things I wish I could do again, things I didn't think to do.

Join the local international adoption support group. You will get lots of support and plenty of invaluable advice on traveling to get your baby and being a parent to an adopted child.

Learn more about your child's country, customs and culture. Find out what kind of clothing and behavior is appropriate.

Learn some of the native language of your child. I wish I had. If there aren't any classes in your area, there are excellent phrasebooks, videos and audiotapes for sale in most bookstores.

Take a parenting class, if one is available in your area. In some locations there are even adoptive parenting classes. Ask your social worker or family doctor for suggestions.

Get your child's room ready.

Childproof your home. Install safety gates, childproof latches and outlet blockers. Securely store out of reach paints, cleaners and other toxic products, prescription and over-the-counter drugs. Crawl around your house at kid level and look for trouble.

Get some regular exercise. It helps reduce stress and boost your energy. Consider yoga or tai chi chuan.

Keep a diary or journal for the baby. If you've never tried writing, take a creative writing class.

Consider volunteering somewhere you can work with children. It's good experience and can help ease your longing to nurture someone.

If you already have children, spend extra time with them. They may be thrilled about getting a new brother or sister, but it's still a good idea to reassure them how much you love them and how special they are.

Spend some time alone with your partner, if you have one. If you don't have children, these are your last weeks alone as a couple.

I learned the value of talking to other parents who are waiting and who've already adopted. It helps to see the "happy ending." Friends and family who haven't experienced adoption can't completely understand. Other adoptive parents do, and they can reassure you that your social worker really isn't the evil twin of your diabolical gym teacher from seventh grade.

And remember, these are the last months you'll ever sleep late or well — for the next few years of your life.

Journal

July 22, 1997

PATIENCE MAKES good parents, the Chinese say. That's what Jennifer Dawson at Children's Bridge told me. I hope there are some other qualities that make good parents because I'm short on patience. Nothing ever happens fast enough for me. I do two things at once all the time. Sometimes I do three.

Martin, our instructor, has us meditate sometimes at the end of our tai chi class. When he says, "Empty your mind," I always want to say, "Where am I supposed to put everything?"

The home study is ready. We're going to Saint John on Thursday to check it, just to make sure there aren't any factual errors. And I feel as though I've swallowed something that's trying to chew its way out of my stomach.

I bought the baby a pair of slippers while we were away. They were in a little shop down by the wharf. I kept going back and picking them up, picturing them on her little feet, and finally Pat said, "Why don't you just buy them?" As ridiculous as it sounds, it hadn't occurred to me I could do that.

July 24, 1997

Judy said lots of terrific things about us in the home study. She described us as "mature and responsible." My first thought was, "Fooled them!"

The home study was fifteen-and-a-half pages long. Judy discussed each of us in turn: our families, our careers, the serious relationships we'd both had. She talked about our marriage: what we'd said about each other and what she'd observed. She said we complemented one another's strengths and weaknesses. Then she talked about our decision to adopt and what we'd told her about how we would deal with the potential problems. I was most interested in the last paragraph: "The writer supports this couple's application for international adoption." All I could think was, we did it.

July 31, 1997

Dorothy Frazier called. The home study won't be presented to Adoption

Services before September 8. Everyone is on vacation. Judy will have to explain all the things she said about us in her report and convince everyone that we are fine, upstanding, responsible people who would make terrific parents.

I tried not to scream when I hung up the phone.

Judy told us that Health and Community Services need to ensure that the baby is coming to a good home. If we were having a biological child, they wouldn't even be involved. Most people don't need anyone's permission to have a child. Just because we're adopting I have to prove I'm good enough.

August 21, 1997

I'm no longer entertaining fantasies of taking the staff of Health and Community Services hostage until they deal with my home study. This time I don't have my hands on the controls. I'm not even in the cockpit. I don't know who is in charge — God, fate or Adoption Services, but it's not me. (It should be me, but apparently I'm the only one who knows that.)

This morning we listed our house for sale. This afternoon we met with Bob Clarke who is going to design our new house.

It's been the kind of day that makes the inside of my head feel as though there is a hamster inside running very fast on a little wheel. I thought I would feel happy about the new house. Instead I feel overwhelmed. My stomach has been driving me crazy.

August 25, 1997

I have our first floor plan. I made paper furniture and played around with it to make sure all of our stuff would fit. (I even made a little paper me and a little paper Pat and a little paper baby.)

I didn't realize how much I'm going to miss the neighbors here, especially Pearl next door. I know this is a lousy time to have second thoughts but since I didn't think things to death beforehand, it seems I'm doing it now.

August 27, 1997

I can't stand all the feelings that waiting brings out in me. I get frantic, desperate and mean-spirited. I think evil thoughts and eat too much chocolate

chocolate-chip ice cream.

Today I found out that the wait to get the baby would be about nine months from the time our papers go to China. Our home study won't be presented and approved until next month. And then it has to go to the provincial coordinator before it even gets sent off to be translated. And on and on and on.

If one more person says, "It's not really that long," I'm going to scream. People who can make a baby don't understand any of this, and I wish they would stop saying they do.

And I can't remember the baby's name. I don't know if I have a crossed circuit in my brain, or if this is some kind of passive act of rebellion to the name Serena. I haven't been able to sell Pat on Grace. And we agreed we'd pick a name we both liked. The only thing we agree on is Claire for her middle name. (I can remember that.)

So we're starting again. It's taking a lot of mental energy not to turn this into a competition.

September 1, 1997

We went up to the lot and made an outline of the house with stakes and string. It looks enormous. People keep saying we'll need a lot more room once we have the baby. They make it sound as though we're getting an elephant instead of a child.

It seems every decision I make now is "for the baby." I wanted the house angled on the lot, partly shaded by the trees. Now it's parallel to the street. More natural light, for the baby. I wanted cozy bedrooms. Now they're big. More space, for the baby. (She's probably about two feet long. How much space does she need?) I don't even have my sun porch. It made the bedroom and living room too dark *for the baby*. I want our child to have a home she'll be happy and safe in, but couldn't she do that in a house with a porch?

My life is changing and I have this compulsion to change everything around me. But I think this change is a mistake. I don't want to build this house. I'm not sure this is a good time for this project. Maybe it would be better to stay in the house we already have. It feels like home to me.

September 8, 1997

I'm proofreading a manuscript for another writer. I think my own hideous spelling is getting better. Being busy with something unrelated to the adoption is good. I don't worry so much and it makes the time go by faster.

We still need to have our home study presented to Adoption Services here. It makes me crazy not knowing when they're going to get moving. Some days I want to go and scream "Move it!" at the entire office — which wouldn't make me look like great mother material.

September 20, 1997

It took some time and I had to wrestle Pat to the floor and sit on him, but we have it narrowed down to two names for the baby: Haley and Lauren. One day I like one and the next day I like the other. On the plus side, at least I can remember both of them.

I can't decide whether it's better to obsess over the baby's name or about when the home study's going to be presented. So I try to do a little of both every day.

My tai chi instructor talks about living in the moment, about finding the joy in where we are right now. And I could do that — if they'd just hurry up with the damn home study.

September 25, 1997

Now it's three names — add Kira to the list — but I swear we're going to pick one.

I've been thinking a lot in the past few days about what I'll tell the baby about being adopted. I know that I'll tell her we're a family by choice and by love. I'll tell her that we worked hard to bring her into our lives. I don't want to pretend that my daughter's life began with us, that the first months of her life have been erased.

It makes me sad that I won't have anything to tell her about her other mother, and I won't have any way to let her other mother know that her baby is safe and loved. I didn't know my father, but I do know a lot about him from all the people who did. I have an image of him in my mind that's probably only partly like the real man. The baby will probably create some fantasy of her birth mother too.

I think I'll say, "Your birth mother wanted you to have a good life with all the opportunities she couldn't give you. She didn't think about what was best for her. She did what was best for you. That's how you know she loved you."

September 29, 1997

I helped my mother move into her new apartment today — fewer stairs for her. When I got home there was a message from Dorothy on the answering machine. The presentation of the home study is scheduled for October 16. That's more than two weeks away.

"Why doesn't this waiting make *you* crazy?" I asked Pat on the phone.

"What good would it do?" he said. "It won't make anything happen any faster. And I just tell myself she's worth the wait. Anyway, you get crazy enough for both of us."

At least he didn't tell me to be patient.

October 16, 1997

Here is how I am today. I opened a can of tomato-rice soup for lunch, poured it down the sink and for a moment couldn't figure out why the soup wasn't in the pot.

There are days my brain goes for a walk and leaves my body to its own devices.

I'm working on the application forms from Citizenship and Immigration. The pile is more than half an inch thick. They want copies of our birth and marriage certificates, a copy of the approval letter from Health and Community Services, letters from our employers, copies of pay stubs and our last year's tax returns. Doing this gives me the illusion that I have some control over when I'm finally going to see my daughter.

At least the baby has a name. We've made our final, final choice. Her name is Lauren Claire Ryan.

October 18, 1997

Judy called with the good news. The home study has been approved. It meets all the province's requirements. I feel wild, as though I'd had three cups of coffee and half a chocolate cake. I should hear from Health and Community Services in a few days about picking up all the paperwork, including our letter of approval, which officially states our home study is satisfactory.

I called Pat in Moncton and we kept saying, "This is good," back and forth to each other on the phone.

November 4, 1997

The official, approved copy of the home study came in the mail today from Health and Community Services. I knew what it was as soon as I saw the envelope jammed into the mailbox. For a couple of long moments I couldn't get my breath. Then it hit me. I felt a rush of exhilaration spread through my chest and down my arms, like I was some junkie scoring a hit.

I called Jennifer at Children's Bridge and got detailed instructions for getting all the papers for our China dossier notarized. (The notary page with the red sticker and the notary seal goes on the front of each group of documents. And then each page has to be embossed with the seal.) I talked to Karen Williamson, our lawyer, who is going to do that. I pulled out all the papers and checked to see what else I needed to get copied. Then I thought about what all this means and I had to sit on the floor because the rush was gone and I had spaghetti knees.

November 10, 1997

I have a pain right behind both eyes. I think there's a real chance I've blown some pathway in my brain. I'm pretty sure I've lost all my reasoning ability and the thirteen times table.

Karen came this morning, and between us I think we have all the papers sealed and notarized the way they're supposed to be. The notary page is in the correct place and every page is embossed with Karen's seal. It all looks very official. Maybe that's all that matters.

Sometimes I'm hit by a feeling, like a big wave rolling over my head, that I will never get through this maze of paper and rules. When that happens, I play the five-minutes-more game. I tell myself I'm only going to put up with all this crap for five more minutes and then I'm throwing in the towel. And when the five minutes are up I decide, okay, I'll give it another five minutes but that's absolutely all I can take. Somehow I convince myself to stand it for another five and another five and I make it through the bad parts.

November 13, 1997

I don't think there are any real people left working for the government. I think there are just rooms full of computers and answering machines. Well, maybe there's one person who dusts once a week.

I couldn't find a real person to give me the courier address so I can send the immigration application. The only number I had was one with automated choices, none of which involved talking to a real person. I went through the entire menu twice and finally tried number five, which was "If you need general information or if you have a complaint." Well, I needed the courier address and my complaint was that I couldn't find a real person to talk to. I pressed five and was immediately disconnected. Okay, so it's funny now. When it happened, I said exactly the same thing the contractor said during the bathroom renovation when he found out the sink wasn't going to fit.

We were at Health and Community Services at 8:30 this morning. I wanted to put our dossier for China directly in Dorothy's hands. Adoption Services will send it to Children's Bridge. The sooner our paperwork gets to them, the sooner it can be translated and sent to China.

Dorothy was out on emergency leave. And my first thought was one hundred percent selfish: *But she can't be out. She has to take care of my adoption papers.* As soon as I thought it, I felt guilty.

So I didn't cry and fling myself on the floor, or make faces, or stomp my feet, or even sigh dramatically. The receptionist promised to put the envelope on Dorothy's desk and I decided to trust her. Not that I had a lot of other good choices.

"This adoption could really happen," I said to Pat last night. "Do you ever get scared thinking about how different life is going to be?"

"I've been asked that a couple of times," he said. "I guess it looks like a pretty drastic change to people. But I'm not scared. I want to do this. There's no going back to my old life, to that person I used to be because I'm not that man anymore. I don't want to be." After a moment he said, "What about you?"

"I just have a huge, overall sense of panic," I said. "About everything."

He patted my arm. "I know, baby," he said. "That's just who you are."

November 14, 1997

I came home and found a message from Jennifer on our machine. She wanted to know where our China dossier was in the system. I called back to tell her it was stuck until at least next Thursday. She's hoping to put together a group of files to send to China about the middle of December and, if everything gets there on time and is done correctly, we could make it into that group. But it doesn't look like we will.

More waiting.

I hung up the phone and cried. Pat sat next to me on the bed and rubbed my back and neither one of us said anything.

November 21, 1997

I decided patience is overrated. I called Dorothy to make sure she received our dossier. Everything allegedly goes to the provincial coordinator on Monday. She'll add our letter of approval. I stressed in the nicest way that I wanted everything sent to Children's Bridge by courier and I was happy to pay. The postal strike has started. Both sides are either talking, or talking about talking, or talking about not talking. I'm not sure which.

November 22, 1997

We've taken our house off the market. No more new house plans. No more little paper sofas and tables. This is a decision I feel happy about.

Pat says he doesn't care where we live and I believe him. All he wants is a good reading lamp, a shower that works and someone else (me) to mow the lawn.

I think I've been in this new house frenzy (my friend Heather calls it my life improvement kick) because it was something I could improve. I don't know how to remake myself into the perfect mother. When I told that to Heather she said, "Jesus, will you just relax. You're already a good mother. You mother everyone around you."

I keep thinking about what she said. Maybe she's right. I've been collecting strays forever. People who wouldn't otherwise have friends, Heather calls some of them. (What does that say about her?) Maybe I already have what it takes.

November 30, 1997

I'm certain some kind of nesting instinct is kicking in. I thought that only happened to pregnant women, but maybe it's something dangling off an X chromosome instead.

I sent Pat back to Moncton with two little pieces of the fabric I want for the curtains in the baby's room. I told him to just walk into Fabricville and look pathetic and someone would help him.

I look around the house and what's been good enough for us isn't good enough for my baby. I want things as close to perfect as I can manage for her. At least now I realize "perfect" doesn't have to be a big fancy house.

I crack-filled and painted Lauren's closet. I bought this huge tub of drywall compound. Standing in the hardware store it seemed really important to have enough. I now have enough to repair the Sheetrock in five houses.

My mother finished the rug she was making for Lauren. It's beautiful: three teddy bears on a white background with a green border. The room's color scheme is turning out to be green and purple. I never thought about pink. I never planned a color scheme. I bought a cute piece of fabric and made a pillow. Maybe subconsciously I was rejecting sexual stereotyping and traditional gender roles for my daughter. Or maybe I just wanted to make a pillow.

December 9, 1997

All the paperwork arrived safely at Children's Bridge. We'll be able to make it into the next group they put together. There will probably be five or six families altogether. All we have to do now is wait until they tell us we have a baby.

I've been so sure that I'd do a piece of the paperwork wrong. It's never been more important for me to do something right. And I've always thought it was important to do everything right. At the end I was even tortured about the right way to staple the pages — should the staple go in horizontal or on an angle? It seemed like something that could make or break our application being approved.

When I went to the mail there was a letter from Immigration saying that our sponsorship application has been approved. Somebody's going to want more paperwork somewhere, I'm sure, before this is over, but I'm not going to think about that now. I was so happy I danced all around the house in my underwear and red sweat-socks singing, "I'm feeling kinda lucky tonight."

December 15, 1997

This morning I went to the library and found China in the National Geographic atlas. I picked out different cities and tried to say their names and wondered if one of them is my daughter's home.

I've been so needy and neurotic I haven't thought about what this has been like for Pat. He goes off to Moncton to work for five days and he never knows what kind of a crazy woman he's coming home to. Sometimes I'd be happy. Sometimes I'd be in tears. Maybe I'd have decimated a closet. But he's never gotten angry and he always comes home. If I'd had to come home to me there would've been days I'd have driven right on past the turn for the bridge.

"Do you think I'm too old to do this?" I asked Pat a few days ago.

"No," he said. "I'm older than you are."

"Does it bother you?"

He shook his head. "I've thought about it quite a bit, but no, not anymore. I think if I'd had a child when I was younger I might have wanted to be out doing other things instead of being home. But I've done a lot of them by now."

He made a hurry-up gesture with one hand. "Remember that show with Gene Wilder?"

"*Something Wilder*," I said.

"Yeah. There was a scene at kindergarten or something. One of the fathers said, 'I had my kids when I was twenty-five.' And Gene's character said, 'I had mine when I was ready.' Well, I'm ready."

December 24, 1997

Happy Christmas, baby.

Next Christmas our daughter will be here. I can already imagine her decorating the tree, singing Christmas carols, making cookies, opening presents. She'll be part of every Christmas and every special moment I have for the rest of my life. I'm always going to have a reason to be happy, as long as I have her.

I keep thinking about the first Christmas tonight. Was the stable warm? Did Joseph hold Mary's hand? Was she scared? Did she look at her baby and wonder if she would be good enough?

I've been thinking about Lauren's birth mother too. Is the baby even born yet? Is my child's other mother hugging her growing belly, longing to keep her baby? Or has she already had to say goodbye? I hope she's somewhere warm and safe when the baby comes. I hope someone holds her hand. I hope she isn't too scared. I wish she could know I'll protect our daughter with my life and I'll love her with all I am.

If my baby is already born, I hope she's warm and safe tonight with enough to eat and someone to watch over her until I get there.

January 7, 1998

My way to relax is to manically clean the house: scrub floors, pull out the furniture, take the toilet seat apart and disinfect it. Sometimes after I've cleaned everything and I still feel crazy, I think about knocking on the neighbors' doors and saying, "Hi. Do you mind if I sanitize your toilet?"

So, I had this big container of drywall compound and there was this crack in the ceiling in Lauren's room, and I'd done such a good job in the closet. And it did seem like a good idea at the time.

As soon as I started scraping away the old flakes of paint from the crack, pieces of the ceiling started falling on the floor — and my head. It didn't make sense to stop then. By the time I was done the crack was about four-and-a-half or five feet long and more than an inch wide in places.

I think there's a lesson in this. I'm just not sure if it's about persistence or stupidity.

January 21, 1998

Gong Xi Fa Cai. That's Happy New Year in Mandarin. At least I think it is. It could be Chinese for "Gee, your hair looks stupid."

The crack on the ceiling is taped and I've put on four coats of compound. Maybe when the baby gets here, I'll take up crack filling for a living. I think writer/broadcaster/crack-filler would look good on a business card. Call me a Renaissance woman.

February 3, 1998

In two days, I'm going to be 40. And I have this feeling of doom, like I'm going to wake up and find I turned into an old fogey overnight. I never thought I'd be a mother for the first time at 40, although if the baby's already born, technically I became a mother at 39.

I got a parcel for my birthday from my sister Maureen today. Inside, along with my present, was one of her handmade teddy bears. I just stood in the middle of the kitchen holding it. It's so beautifully made and so unexpected.

I wasn't sure what Maureen would think about our decision to adopt. She is my big sister and I guess I did want her approval. Now I feel I have it.

February 25, 1998

We are in Group 51. The list of people who are in the group with us, five families altogether, came today from Children's Bridge, plus our copy of the translation.

I looked at all the symbols and tried to figure out which one meant which English word. I can imagine someone who only knows Mandarin looking at all our papers in English and trying to do the same thing. When something doesn't make sense to a Chinese person does he throw up his hands and say, "It might as well be English?"

March 21, 1998

The travel guide arrived from Children's Bridge. Twenty pages. Everything from travel etiquette to a detailed list of what to pack. I read it twice, but I can't remember what I'm supposed to buy. Maybe it's not my stomach that's stopped working properly. Maybe it's my brain.

I'm learning that even if you're scared and you think you can't do something, as long as you keep getting up in the morning and going forward, you will get what you need in the end. It doesn't mean you stop being afraid. You just drag the fear along with you, like a sack at the end of a piece of rope. Until some day you realize it wore out, or you lost it. Suddenly the fear is gone and you've made it.

John McAdam offered to go over the packing list with us so we'd know what they found useful and what they could have lived without. I wrote all over my copy. *Take plenty of Kleenex. Buy extra fuses for the adaptor. Take a hotpot. Pepto-Bismol and Neo-citran. Zip-lock bags. Small garbage bags. Take tampons even if you think you won't need them. Pack copies of the baby's picture. An inflatable back cushion for the plane. Use the hotel laundry.*

March 27, 1998

It was warm enough to work outside this afternoon, so I started taking the old paint off my rocking chair. I've had it since I was six. I think it was scavenged from the dump. I hope that doesn't bother Lauren.

It's like digging for buried treasure, seeing what's under each layer of paint. I remember the cream color under the green that was on top. I found a pale blue under that and under the blue I discovered the chair was originally stained and varnished. I tried to picture a different child for each color.

Such a nice thing happened today, too. Our neighbor, Pearl, came out while I was working and said, "I'd like to buy the crib for the baby." I can't let her. They're way too expensive, but it feels so wonderful that she wants to.

April 8, 1998

I can't sleep. There's a tube up my nose with a probe hanging from the end, measuring the pH at the top of my stomach. The rest of the tube is taped to my cheek and neck. It attaches to a recorder box that I'm wearing across my body like a purse. When I try to eat, the tube moves in my nose as though my stomach is trying to suck the entire thing inside.

This is supposed to help the doctors figure out what's causing all the heartburn I get. Sometimes I have attacks of pain so bad I've ended up in the emergency room with my throat frozen. I've had so much stuff shoved down my throat I think I'm ready for a gig as a sword swallower.

This stomach problem has been going on for months and months and I don't have any patience left. I'm not very patient at the best of times. And what I had I used getting all the adoption paperwork done. I don't want to have to be on guard over every bite of food that goes into my mouth. I don't want to keep trying different drugs hoping the next one will turn out to be my "magic elixir."

How can I go to China with all this pain? I can't take care of a baby there or here like this.

I'm in the hospital hostel, which is just some rooms at the end of one floor. The only people I've seen tonight are a security guard and the teenager in the room across the hall. I watched her sneak out over an hour ago. And I'm thinking I could walk down to the lobby and call a taxi. I could go home and slide into bed next to Pat and come back again very early and no one would know.

April 24, 1998

Lauren's crib is going to be delivered tomorrow. It's maple, a very simple, beautiful design. I liked it the moment I saw it.

Pearl wanted to do this, and even though I feel it's extravagant, she wouldn't take no for an answer.

She invited me to go to lunch because I'd helped her move some furniture. When we came out and got in the car Pearl said, "Now we're going to look at cribs." I said, "We are not." She ignored me.

I've been trying to get rid of anything that might be dangerous to the baby — or at least get it out of the way. I put all the paint and scrapers up in my new basement cupboard. I stuck outlet blockers in every plug in the house. I put safety catches on all the cupboards. Then I crawled around the house looking for trouble from a baby's eye-view.

Mostly all I found was dust.

April 29, 1998

Pat and I put the crib together this afternoon. I couldn't wait and I bugged him until he couldn't wait.

I'm saving this crib forever. My first grandchild is going to sleep in this crib.

April 30, 1998

It's my mother's birthday today. We had a wonderful party at the Sheraton Hotel. Maureen came from Halifax and all of my mother's friends were there. I'm feeling very self-satisfied and I probably look like the Cheshire cat, nothing but grin.

One of the women at the party said, "You know as soon as you adopt you'll get pregnant. It always happens." I just smiled. It's not going to happen this time, and if it did, I'd have a lot of explaining to do.

Dr. Koller has changed the medication for my stomach. I have less pain, but I'm tired all the time. I feel as though I'm trying to move through a bowl full of Jell-O.

I don't believe medication is a solution anymore. But I think I might have found one. I saw a doctor on the *Today Show* discussing an operation that can help people, like me, who have acid reflux disease. I went to the library and looked it up in the *Merck Manual.* When I saw Dr. Koller I said, "I want someone to operate and fix this for good." It came out more adamant than I'd intended.

He almost smiled. "All right. I'll send you to a surgeon," he said. "I'd like to hear what he'll say."

My appointment is next week. I don't care what the surgeon says, as long as he fixes me before we leave for China to get the baby.

May 9, 1998

Pat's parents gave me his baby dishes. There's a cup, a bowl and a plate. They're just like new. Either he didn't use them much or he was a very well behaved baby, because they don't look as though they've been tossed off a high chair very often.

I've been making Lauren a teddy bear and I can't seem to get the feet pads to go in no matter what I do. What am I going to do? How am I going to put diapers and sleepers and those one-piece underwear things on a baby when I can't even get two goddamn foot pads in a teddy bear?

May 18, 1998

I woke up just after three and I knew how to fix the teddy bear's feet, so I got out of bed and drew a picture of what I wanted to do on the back of a Zellers receipt because I couldn't find any paper. And it worked.

When I was about two my dad made me a teddy bear. My mother says I took one look at it and screamed. I never did play with it, but it's gone everywhere I've gone.

My dad's been dead a long time, but I always miss him when something good happens. Or maybe what I miss is what I think it would be like to have a father, because I don't remember him at all. I think he'd be happy about us adopting a baby. Mum said he loved kids.

I think I must look fragile to everyone, as though I might suddenly sit down on the sidewalk and burst into tears. Now when I meet anyone they ask me in a gentle voice, "Is it okay to ask about the baby?" I always say yes. Right now there's nothing to tell.

May 22, 1998

I read somewhere that the adoption process is supposed to be my "pregnancy." I've now been "pregnant" for fifteen months and I don't have a clue when I'm going to see my daughter. If I were really pregnant this would probably get me on the cover of a tabloid and a sweeps special on Fox.

I ran into a friend, Marsha Davis, in the parking lot of the Superstore. I haven't seen her in a long time and when she asked "What's new?" I said, "Pat and I are adopting a baby from China."

"That's wonderful," she said. Then she did a double take and her mouth sort of hung open. "Pat?" she exclaimed. "I mean it's wonderful, but Pat?"

He laughed when I told him. "It'll do people good to shake them up a little," he said.

May 30, 1998

Since we're not moving I've decided I need somewhere to put my lawn mower and clippers and rakes and all the other clutter. The contractor arrived this morning with two guys from his crew and the hole is ready to pour the slab for my new garden shed. I made them coffee, then hung over the railing of the side steps and whistled at them while they were digging.

Early this morning I went to a yard sale at the College Hill Daycare and found a perfect changing table for Lauren. There was no way it would fit in the car, but I figured that I could swipe the contractor's truck while the guys were digging, because I know where he leaves the keys. Then one of the people working at the sale offered to drive it down in his truck for me. It just felt as though I was meant to have that table.

June 4, 1998

I like to get up in the morning and go into the baby's room. I stand at the foot of her crib and try to imagine what it will be like when she's there to smile back at me.

Mum and I have been baby shopping. If I just looked at something she'd say, "You need it," and throw it in the cart.

I need to get ready now, because I'm going to have the stomach surgery. The surgeon, Dr. Peters, is going to do a Nissen fundoplication. He'll wrap my stomach around my esophagus to tighten the valve. That should get rid of the pain and the horrible heartburn.

Dr. Peters said I'm a good candidate for the surgery and this should work. I told him it has to. I have to be able to go to China and not get sick there. He has an adopted child and I think he understands.

It wasn't an easy decision. I'm extremely vain. Surgery means a scar. Well, five little tiny ones. But they're still scars. And I'm afraid he'll have a resident sew me up — some little twerp who probably couldn't truss a turkey.

June 8, 1998

I realize I'm way out of sync with my friends. They have teen-agers; I'll have a baby. They'll be worrying about paying for university. I'll be worrying about potty training.

I was out of sync before we started this. When you don't have kids, people think you don't like them. They're afraid you'll be bored by school plays and dance recitals. That you'll be annoyed by small people who are only eating Cheerios and lint. And maybe some people without children do feel that way. I never did.

Maybe that was already a hint of the big change coming.

Every night before I go to bed I look out at the night sky and I think it's the same sky over me that's over my baby. And then she doesn't seem quite so far away.

June 25, 1998

"Will you know anything about the baby?" I've been asked more than once. Why does that matter to some people? Not knowing anything about my daughter doesn't scare me. Not getting to be a mother does.

I wish we could know some of her birth family's medical history. And I'd like to be able to tell Lauren something about her birth mother. I'd like to be able to say, "You have her eyes and her smile." I'd like to meet the woman who gave birth to my child. I'd like to say thank you to her, although there should be a bigger word than that. Thank you seems so small and simple for what she's giving me.

But I truly don't care about anything else. What more would I know about her if we had made her? I don't know what mix of DNA we would have created. (There are some odd people in my family.)

July 9, 1998

I am so close to having everything I have ever wanted that sometimes it feels as fragile as a bubble resting on my hand. It's so beautiful, so perfect that I'm afraid I'll do the wrong thing and it'll break.

John McAdam called to say there is a chance that our group may get put together with group 50. If that happens, we could get our referral in about a month and we could be on our way to China by the end of September.

"Don't get your hopes up," John said. I was trying to be nice, but I got off the phone as fast as I could because I was starting to hyperventilate. I told him I'd keep it all in perspective, then as soon as I hung up I had to sit on the floor with my head between my knees because I really couldn't breathe.

July 14, 1998

I've painted the rocking chair pale pink and made chair pads to match the curtains. It's not easy distracting myself from thinking about September.

I talked to the public health nurse today and made the appointment for our immunizations at the travel clinic. We need to have hepatitis A and B, plus typhoid and tetanus shots. And of course there will be a form to fill out.

Sometimes I wonder if other people get as scared about all this as I do. Once in a while, I am hit with this feeling, like being pulled out into deep water by the current. I feel like I'm way over my head and there's nowhere solid to put my feet down.

I don't want the baby ever to be sorry that she ended up with me.

July 30, 1998 (From the hospital)

I have a tube down my nose, a catheter in my bladder and an IV in one arm. (I look like a whiskey still.) They make me walk down to the elevator and back so I won't get blood clots. I have to drag along the morphine pump and my IV pole and I'm hunched over like a gorilla.

I have a nice, new stomach valve. I also have five scars on my stomach. I hate them.

Pat talked to Dorothy Frazier. She has something from China — I don't know what. I told him to come directly to the hospital from Dorothy's office. I don't care what time visiting hours start. I have a bag of pee and I'm not afraid to use it.

July 31, 1998 (From the hospital)

I started watching for Pat at 8:30. I shuffled along the same strip of hallway at least a dozen times, past the nurses' desk, past the old guy sitting in his johnny shirt with his scrotum hanging out, past the laundry cart.

Pat finally arrived, just as I was about to do lap number twelve past the nurses' station. Even in my doped state I felt a rush of excitement. Dorothy had given Pat a copy of the adoption offer from China, the baby's medical report and a tiny, very fuzzy faxed picture of her. There'll be papers to sign and a photo on August 4. All the adoption offer says is that they have a baby for us. Her Chinese name is Wu Jian Ying. She's eleven months, older than we expected, but I don't care. She's in an orphanage in Wuzhou, which is in southern China. I could barely make out her face in the fax but I couldn't stop looking at the page.

Dr. Peters eventually came in to see me and said I could go home as long as I followed his instructions. I just nodded at everything he said. I don't have a clue what promises I've made.

August 2, 1998

Now that I'm home I feel a bit better, although I can't even roll over in bed by myself. Pat has to sleep on the floor because I can't stand to have the bed move. Two of my scars are crooked.

But in two more days I'm going to see a photo of my daughter's beautiful face.

August 4, 1998

Everything is rosy pink. Which might have something to do with the four Dilaudid I had today. Dorothy called late this morning to ask us to come by her office. I told Pat, "Don't even try to leave me home." But when he fastened my seatbelt, I had to start chewing my tongue so I wouldn't moan.

When Dorothy gave me the baby's picture, I forgot how to talk. My baby is so beautiful. I forgot how bad I felt. I forgot where I was. We signed the offer saying that we want to be her parents and I struggled for a moment to think of my name and remember how to make the letters. I couldn't stop staring at that little picture.

We decided to keep one of the baby's Chinese names. So now her name is Lauren Jian Claire Ryan.

When we got home, Pat called his mom and dad and Bob and Rhonda. I talked to my mother for a few minutes and Heather too. Heather's heard me whine about every bit of crappy news. She deserves to be in on the good stuff as well.

I can't stop thinking about Lauren. Is she all right? Now that I can see her face I have ten times the worries. She looks like she's been well taken care of from the picture. I guess I'm going to have to have faith.

Belief in things unseen. Not easy for me.

August 6, 1998

Things I did today:

    1. Sat up

    2. Didn't puke

I'm trying to get everything ready to send back to Children's Bridge. I'm so slow and unfocused, it's like my brain keeps floating away. I hope I'll feel better soon. I have to start thinking about the trip to China.

I saw our family doctor today. She said I'm healing well. I asked her about a checkup for Lauren when we come back from China. She said to bring the baby in as soon as we get back and she'll check her over and set up any tests Lauren will need at the hospital.

August 11, 1998

We had our first immunizations today: hepatitis A and B. I'm not moving around any faster, but I feel better.

I now know a lot more about malaria than I used to. That's because what I knew came from watching old movies. The hero would get bitten by a mosquito, stagger around for a quarter of the movie, and then someone would finally say, "My God, man, you're burning up!" I didn't even know malaria was treatable with antibiotics.

Old movies are not a good source of information.

August 13, 1998

Last night we went to a meeting the McAdams had organized because Martha Maslen, the social worker from Children's Bridge, is here.

I'm glad we went to the meeting, even though I was so exhausted when we got home I was shaking. Everyone there has either already been through this process or is somewhere in the midst of it. Everyone else in my life has been wonderful, especially considering how irrational I've been some days, but they don't understand because they can't. For once I didn't have to explain myself. I could use one or two words instead of three or four paragraphs and see recognition. It's what I need right now.

Today I called Jennifer at the Children's Bridge office to find out what the baby weighs. She's so little; just six-and-a-half kilograms and sixty-five centimeters long. Some of the clothes we bought are going to have to be returned for smaller sizes.

August 16, 1998

We found an umbrella stroller to take to China with us at a yard sale yesterday for only two dollars. I went to the bookstore and spent all the money I saved on *What to Expect: The Toddler Years*. I read the chapter for the eleventh month. I wondered how much of the "should be able to/may be able to" the baby can do.

Mostly, I worry that Lauren won't like me. I've read that it's harder for children who are already a year old to bond. All I know to do is just love her and give her the chance to love me.

All I have is this tiny picture and already so much love waiting to give her. And yet I'm so frightened because I've never cared about anything so much.

August 24, 1998

Finding pristine American money to take with us has turned into an ordeal. (Okay, so everything seems like an ordeal.) Children's Bridge said the money should be clean with no tears or writing on the bills. I struck out at two banks. No one would promise the money wouldn't look like a slobbering St. Bernard had carried it around.

I called Tracey Adams, who is my investment advisor at the Royal Bank, to see if she could think of anything I could do. She said, "What exactly do you need?" I told her and she said, "I'll take care of it." And she did.

I picked up the money today. It looks perfect. Most of the American bills we're taking are for our donation to the orphanage, to reimburse them for taking care of Lauren. Plus there are other fees, like the notary's, to do with the paperwork.

We expect to leave for China in less than a month. I know at some point really soon I'm going to have to stop checking and re-checking and just jump into the unknown.

But not yet.

August 27, 1998

We read the instructions three times. We checked and adjusted and tightened and I think the car seat is installed properly. We picked it out and Pat's mom and dad paid for it. I keep going to the front window and looking to see if it's still in the car.

There's a holdup in someone's paperwork, so we may not leave until September 25. For a few minutes, I was filled with fury, but it passed. I try to remember what Alden Nowlan wrote: *Rage is not a lifetime commitment, but only a passage of darkness in the mind, a cold shiver of the soul."*

September 3, 1998

Yesterday I said to Pat, "Aren't you worried about being able to take care of the baby?"

And he said, "No. I suppose I probably should be. I don't know anything about babies. Maybe it's just that I don't know enough to worry."

No wonder I'm such a mess. I have to be scared for two people.

September 7, 1998

The spare bedroom looks like a giant flea market's about to happen. I have everything we'll need in China for ourselves and for the baby piled at one end of the room. We bought two of the biggest suitcases I've ever seen. I've tried to balance amounts and weights and split what we'll need evenly between the two bags.

I'm great at packing. I'm just lousy at the actual traveling part. I'm about to go to the other side of the world and I'm terrified. But I'm just going to go ahead and do it anyway.

Fortunately, all I have to do today is start deciding how to pack the suitcases.

September 10, 1998

Lauren is a year old today. Next year at this time we'll be celebrating her birthday together.

Paul Chee-a-tow, the leader of the combined groups, called to say we will be leaving on October 2. There will be seventeen couples traveling altogether. Part of the group will be going to Wuzhou. The rest will head to Nancheng.

Pat and I will fly to Vancouver and spend the night there. I think most of the other couples will be doing the same thing. The flight to Beijing leaves Vancouver at lunchtime. Twelve hours in the air and we'll be there.

September 17, 1998

I'm running out of things to do. This is not good. I keep thinking about the trip and scaring myself even more. We'll be going from Nanning to Wuzhou by bus. Twelve hours with the babies.

What if she really doesn't like me? Who knows what goes on in a baby's mind anyway? What if she takes one look at me and says to herself, "I don't think so. Send that one back to the Mommy Store."

Sometimes I think I'm just looking for ways to drive myself crazy.

September 27, 1998

A week from now I'll be in China. I've been saying that to people, just trying out the sound of the words. I'm very casual, like going halfway around the world is something I do all the time, when really I'm petrified.

We'll be one night in Beijing, three days in Nanning to take care of the last bit of paperwork, and two days in Wuzhou. We'll get the baby's passport in Wuzhou. Then we'll fly back to Beijing for the second week. All the babies will need to have medicals and then we have to wait for their visas from the Canadian embassy. I don't have a clue when we'll actually see the baby. Maybe as soon as we get to Nanning.

I started packing today. All I care about is getting everything in for Lauren. And my curling iron. It's always been one of my rules for life that I never go anywhere I can't take my curling iron.

September 28, 1998

Everything is packed with a little room to spare. There are enough diapers, formula and baby cereal for more than two weeks. Clothes for Lauren. Clothes for us. A few toys. Plus the hotpot, my curling iron, and the adaptor. I'm ready. All evening I've had panic attacks where I couldn't remember if I put something in the correct bag and then I'd have to go look for whatever it was. So far I've searched for the juice cup, diapers, bottle bags, suppositories and a hat.

And I ironed the money.

I used just a little steam and ironed out the odd fold mark. It makes the money look a little bit more crisp and perfect, and how can that hurt?

September 30, 1998

We leave tomorrow.

I think my butterflies are big enough to get me there without a plane.

Stage Four:
THE TRIP ABROAD

The trip to get your child is an incredible experience. It may be your first experience in another culture. If this is your first child, you leave home as a single person or as a couple and come back as a family.

If you've never traveled outside your own country you'll probably experience some culture shock. Food, dress, music, language and customs may all be different from your way of life. For me, being surrounded by a language I didn't understand left me feeling homesick.

PRACTICAL ASPECTS

The trip will be easier if you have the things you really need, but at the same time you're not loaded down with luggage. Your adoption facilitator will give you a list of what you should pack. Other parents who have recently been to the same country are a great help too. Ask what they didn't need and what they really wished they had taken.

Before you travel you'll need to have certain immunizations.

Contact the travel clinic run by your provincial public health department. Staff at the travel clinic will know which shots you need and can advise you on things like anti-malarial medication if this disease is a concern where you're traveling.

Check the expiry date on your passport. When we traveled to China, the Chinese Embassy would not issue a visa to anyone whose passport was due to expire in the next six months. Make copies of your passport information and airline tickets. Keep a copy with you and leave a copy with someone at home.

Everyone advised us not to take a lot of luggage. We bought the two biggest suitcases we could find, going on the theory that a couple of huge pieces of luggage would be easier to manage than several small ones. If you don't travel very much, try to borrow suitcases. I later found out a friend had luggage she would have been happy to lend us. Check on the airline's restrictions on the maximum number and weight of bags. If you're going to be flying within your child's country, keep in mind luggage limitations on domestic flights may be different. We each used a large backpack as carry-on luggage. I liked the idea of having my hands free. Most of the others in our group used tote bags, wearing the strap across their bodies.

Take along traveler's checks — ours were in American dollars — and a major credit card. You may need some cash for in-country fees like having documents notarized. Your adoption facilitator will tell you what you should take. If you don't have one already, consider obtaining a long-distance calling card. Make sure you can use it in the country to which you're traveling.

Buy extra health insurance if you don't belong to a plan that will cover you for the duration of your trip. I haven't come across any insurer that will cover your child.

Take along a camcorder, even if you have to borrow one. Images of where your child was born can be a treasured link to your child's birth country. A hotpot, which resembles a small electric kettle, makes it easy to boil water at any time. Don't forget a voltage converter and plug adaptors. Without them you won't be able to charge the battery on your camcorder or use your hotpot.

The specifics of what you should take with you depend on the country in which you are traveling. Your agency can give you suggestions and other adoptive parents will have lots of ideas. You'll probably find most of the items on the following list useful.

Zip-lock bags. There are dozens of uses for them. I carried one full of Cheerios and one with several baby wipes.

Toilet paper. You can pull the cardboard tube out of the center and flatten the roll for easy packing. An adoptive father who traveled to Russia described the toilet paper as "crepe paper."

Small, kitchen size garbage bags. Again, you'll find lots of uses for these. Scented bags are wonderful for dirty diapers.

A folding umbrella stroller. A cranky baby can sometimes be soothed to sleep by being wheeled up and down a hotel hallway. Canadian Airlines supplied us with a large, heavy plastic bag for the stroller.

A Snugli. Lauren hated it, but many of the other babies loved to be carried close to the body.

A small flashlight. You will have to get up in the middle of the night.

Any prescription drugs you take, in their original containers, with childproof caps. Take extras in case your trip is extended.

Money belt or money wallet. We each wore a money belt and Pat also wore an around-the-neck money wallet. We used them for our airline tickets, passports, traveler's checks, credit cards and money.

Decongestant. Lots of it. Both Lauren and I had bronchitis in China.

Duct tape. This is something else for which you'll find lots of uses. Jeff Wilson, a seasoned camper who was part of our travel group, had a roll and very generously let us mooch pieces from him to patch the holes in the stroller bag.

Food. Dry cereal, instant noodle cups, teabags, hot chocolate and coffee bags, along with your hotpot to boil water. This is so you have something to eat in your room, when you're running late or feeling exhausted. You'll need several plastic cups and utensils as well.

Comfortable walking shoes. You'll be on your feet a lot. This is a time to let comfort override style.

FUTURE MEMORIES

Most parents try to bring back mementos for their children. We chose a few toys Lauren could play with right away, as well as several gifts to give her when she's older. Some parents in our travel group bought gifts for each one of their daughter's future birthdays, up to age eighteen. These remembrances are another good way to make your child's heritage part of her new life.

Take lots of film and extra batteries for your camera, plus a small notebook to record your feelings and memories. These thoughts and photos can be the basis of a memory book for your child, a scrapbook of images and remembrances of her birthplace. Consider also taking along a small instant camera. You'll be able to leave pictures of you and your child with the people who cared for her.

Try to see as much as you can of the place where your child was born. Videotape everything. Write down your impressions. You can't capture textures, scents or feelings on tape. You may not always be able to answer your child's questions about her beginnings, but you can give her the chance to see what her first home was like.

Don't miss the chance to talk to your child's caregivers. Ask about his favorite foods, toys and games. Find out about his eating and sleeping schedule. Remember to say thank you to everyone who has looked after your little one. If it's allowed, ask for the information you need to stay in touch and offer to send pictures. I've kept in contact with my daughter's nanny from the orphanage, Chen Ping. Several times a year, we write to each other and send photographs. It's a small way of keeping connected with Lauren's first home. As well, I could see how much Chen Ping cared about Lauren. It seemed cruel to completely cut their ties.

The Emotional Challenges

Preparing for your trip mentally, anticipating possible problems and planning how you'll deal with them and the inevitable stress you'll experience is a good idea. Ask your adoption facilitator to suggest someone you can talk to who has recently made the same trip. The more facts you have ahead of time, the less daunting the journey will seem. I've never been a good traveler — I'm too attached to my own way of life and my own things. When our group leader told us we were going to be spending twelve hours on a bus traveling from Nanning to Wuzhou, I scared myself, imagining everything that could go wrong from no bathrooms to being stranded in some tiny village. The real trip turned out to be a lot easier than I'd anticipated.

It's important to remember that bureaucracy is the same in every language in every country. Be prepared for delays, small changes to regulations and rules that don't make sense to you. Be gracious and accommodating, something I sometimes wasn't and regret very much. Stressed and scared, with a sick child, and feeling ill myself, I was rude and difficult a number of times. The most important thing to take with you when you go to get your child is a positive, flexible, co-operative attitude. Remember that you're a guest in your child's birth country, as well as a representative for your own country and all the adoptive families who will visit after you do.

The families with whom you travel can be a lifeline when you run into problems. Members of our group shared things like bottled water and decongestant with us. If you're lucky enough to travel with accommodating people, let them know you appreciate their help and try to help someone else when you can. From this shared experience you may forge close relationships that will continue once you return home. Do consider that other parents are tired and stressed, and may be too emotionally raw from the adoption process to closely connect with others in the group.

You'll probably already be in love with the child you've been creating in your mind all during the adoption process. Try to remember that to your child you're still a stranger, even though she may have been told that mommy and daddy will be coming soon.

I went to China with no expectations of what my daughter would be like. Some children bond quickly and easily with their new parents. That's how it happened for us. I sometimes think all that walking the floor with Lauren, while I sang Ben E. King and Peter, Paul and Mary songs to her as she coughed throughout the night, helped cement our bond. Other little ones, especially those who've been in foster homes, may be distraught over leaving what they consider is their family. These children need time to grieve as well as time to trust you and feel comfortable. Take your cue from your child. Watch her body language and how she responds to you. Don't push physical affection on her if it upsets her. Let her decide if she wants to be held or sit in your lap. She will get closer to you as she comes to know you and to feel safe with you.

Journal

October 1, 1998 (Vancouver)

WE LEFT THE HOUSE at six-thirty for the airport. It was dark and the rain splattered against the car. I'd been awake since four listening to the thunder, alternating between panicking and taking deep breaths as I tried to relax. (I've probably developed the lung capacity of a Japanese pearl diver over the past few months.)

Rhonda and Jennifer met us at the airport to take charge of the car while we're away. Rhonda brought us a care package. She told us to wait until we were bored on the plane to open the bag. I waited until they shut off the seat belt sign. There was Gravol, Tylenol, a decongestant, a Tweety and Sylvester book, some stickers, and even a romance kit with candles, bubble bath and sparkling water. I filled the hotel tub with bubbles and drank the water. I am just too tired for romance.

As the plane climbed, I watched everything get smaller until it all disappeared. I thought, when I come back it will all be the same, but I'll be a different person. I held Pat's hand very tightly. "Scared?" I asked. "Yeah," he said. "But in a good way."

I took out the little picture of Lauren at three months and tried to imagine what she looks like now. Now she's over a year old. I wonder if she's walking or trying to. I wonder if she can say any words. She could have a huge vocabulary. She could be a baby genius. But she'll be babbling in Mandarin. So how would I know?

It was gray and wet in Montreal, the kind of drizzle that makes me feel soggy. As we descended to the airport, we passed over bare fields plowed in for winter and the trees looked like a huge hooked rug in oranges, yellows and scarlet.

The flight to Vancouver was long and cramped. I'm thinking we should upgrade to first class between Vancouver and Montreal on the way home. I got us to the right gate in Montreal and to the hotel shuttle in Vancouver. I always start out following other people, but I walk so fast I end up with people following me. It's kind of like being the head lemming.

October 2, 1998 (on the plane)

We're a couple of hours underway. We met Paul Chee-a-tow, our group leader, and some of the other people in the group. I didn't meet everyone; the group is so large — seventeen families.

I think I've already gotten off on the wrong foot. "The group" was heading for the airport hours before we had to board, but I wanted to wash my hair and have breakfast. I'm just not a team player.

(Later)

We flew over the Great Wall. The land all around it is so brown and bare. The wall snakes across the top of the hills like something a child made. The original wall was built by hundreds of thousands of workers more than two thousand years ago. No cranes, no trucks, no bulldozers. Just people.

It was warm when we landed. Not as much smog as I expected but the smell was just like the air would be after a fire. Tonight there is low, gray/orange haze hanging over the city.

From the runway, I couldn't even see the airport terminal. We walked down a canopy-covered set of stairs. A soldier, rigid at attention, stood at the bottom.

There were buses waiting to drive us to the terminal. No seats — just poles and handholds from the ceiling. There were buses, planes, cars, jeeps, trucks, scooters and bicycles moving everywhere on the ramp. The rule seemed to be that the bigger you are the more right of way you have. So we waited in a line more than once, while a plane taxied by right in front of us.

At the terminal they took our arrival slips and looked at our passports and we were waved through customs. I don't know what I expected. To be frisked or have our luggage searched? It's a communist country; I thought someone would at least want to pat my pockets.

Our guide, whose name is Cindy, was waiting with a little yellow flag. We followed her out of the airport to the bus like a line of baby ducks. There was a van for the luggage — the bus was for us. A photo of Mao Zedong with a red plastic flower and a wall clock hung at the front of the bus.

Once we were settled in the hotel Cindy took us to Carrefors, the grocery store down the street, for bottled water. I kept thinking I'm on the other side of the world. There we were in the dark, surrounded by that smoky haze with people and cars everywhere, horns honking, and no words that sounded like home.

The store is about the size of a medium-sized grocery store at home, but I've never been in a store with so many people. They were swarming and talking and staring at us. I stood at the end of an aisle and stared while it all moved around me. It must be where everyone in the neighborhood shops. There are two floors. Food is on the bottom floor and the top floor is like a department store. The signs are in English and Mandarin. It isn't so different from any other grocery store I've been in. There were cans of coke next to the bottled water.

We got our water, paid for it, and made it back to the hotel alone. By this time Cindy was gone. Not my idea of guiding, but it's not my country.

I crossed an intersection in China by myself. Cars were coming from more directions than I could look. Okay, there was a light but not all the traffic stopped when it turned red.

Except for the "Water not for drinking" sign in the bathroom, we could be in a Canadian or American hotel. The traffic continued all night, but it slowed down just after ten and picked up again about six.

There are two beds — three-quarter size. Pat and I slept very close together.

October 4, 1998 (Beijing)

At breakfast we met another couple who will be traveling with us, Cathy and Henry. Their daughter's name is Emma. They showed me her picture and I wondered whether she and Lauren are friends.

The group is splitting up. Ten families, including us, are adopting babies from Wuzhou. The other seven are traveling to Nancheng. We have a new guide until we get back to Beijing. Her name is Louisa. We're on a China Xinhua Airlines jet on the way to Nanning. Nanning is the capital of Guangxi province. Wuzhou, where Lauren is from, is in Guangxi too, farther south. Tomorrow morning or maybe even tonight we'll see our daughter for the first time.

I keep wondering if I packed the right stuff. We only brought one suitcase and the backpacks. The other suitcase stayed behind at the hotel in Beijing.

I've never been anywhere like the Beijing airport. People everywhere, pushing, talking, yelling. Everything goes by very fast, all swirling, moving people, color, motion and so much noise. I couldn't stick out my arm and not touch someone. And I was always on my toes, trying to see.

(Later - Nanning)

It was steamy outside but very green and lush. I felt as though I could grab a handful of air and squeeze the water out.

In each row of seats on our bus there was an extra one — like a jump seat — that folds into the aisle. They're all Noxzema jar blue. At the front there was another photograph of Mao Zedong. I tried to imagine the buses at home with a photo of Jean Chrétien posted at the front. It wouldn't last until lunchtime.

Our local guide's name is Roger. He told me one of his professors gave him the name Roger. I asked Roger what his Chinese name is, but he just shook his head. "Too hard for you to say," he said. His English is excellent and I'm ashamed that I don't even know how to say "please" in Mandarin.

I pressed my face against the window on the way into the city. I wanted to remember everything so I can tell my baby about it all someday.

There was field after field of sugar cane and tall, broad-leaved bamboo trees, but everything had a gray cast to it, as though a layer of dirt or dust had settled over it all.

It's so poor here. We passed huts made of concrete block with corrugated metal roofs. Most places had a small garden plot and there were usually scrawny chickens scratching in the yard and water buffalo standing around. I didn't see any kind of mechanical farm equipment. Life seems to take so much work. It was like turning back time by a hundred years. There is garbage all along the road and people squatting at the edge selling vegetables — a lot of watermelon.

Water buffalo wander all over the place. They stand along the edges of the road. They stand in the road. Once the bus driver had to wait for a herd that filled both lanes of traffic. He blew the horn and kept nudging the bus forward until we could pass. The water buffalo lumbered off as though they were stoned and didn't care.

A lot of people ride bicycles. Old, rusty, junky ones that would have been scrapped at home. Lots of times there was one person pedaling and someone else riding on the handlebars or back fender. Everyone drives very fast here, weaving and cutting so close I kept sucking in my breath, expecting one of those bicycles to get flattened between us and a car, like a mosquito between two clapped hands. And the horns never stop honking; it's part of how they drive. I think there's some kind of code that I haven't figured out yet.

I was trying to follow everything Roger was saying but my attention kept going out the window. Then someone asked if he knew when we'd see the babies. His answer: tonight. People's hearts really do stop beating for a second or two, because I know mine did.

Tonight. All I could think was *I'm not ready*. I'm not ready and why won't this goddamn bus go any faster. I wanted to run up to the front and lay on the horn. I hugged Pat and my stomach felt as though dozens of pterodactyl butterflies were fluttering their wings in there. My eyes were full of tears and I had to lay my head against the seat for a minute to keep them back.

I really don't think I'm ready. What if she hates me? What if she looks at me and screams and won't stop? What if I've forgotten everything I know about babies which I really think I might have because my brain is all over the place at the moment.

(Later)

We got to our hotel, the Wufeng, and by the time we got to our room and received the luggage we had less than an hour before we'd meet our children. Our room isn't very big. There are twin beds and a small, blue metal crib for the baby. I went over every inch of that crib. I yanked all the joints. I pounded on the bottom. There's no mattress. Or bumper pads. I rolled our windbreakers and sweatshirts into makeshift bumper pads. Some part of me always has to keep moving. It seems as though I can hear the buzz of my own nervous energy in my ears.

(Later)

We gathered in the lobby. I had the nanny's gift bag and a tiny stuffed Eeyore for the baby. The babies have been taken care of by "nannies" at the orphanage in Wuzhou. We've brought small gifts for the women, really just a token to say thank you. I packed everything in a pretty gift bag: soap, two bottles of lotion, lipstick, a pair of pantyhose, a little box of chocolates, gummi bears and a pretty hair clip. I'm trying to say thank you to someone who has taken care of my daughter for the past year, but this doesn't seem like enough.

Some of the parents had changed their clothes and put on makeup. I hadn't even brushed my teeth. I felt stupid because I wasn't dressed up for Lauren. I hadn't thought about it. The only thing I could think about was meeting my baby.

Together we followed Paul Chee-a-tow outside, down a side path in the darkness, past a little pond, to a meeting room, bright with lots of lights for the video cameras. I was clutching Pat's hand so hard it must have hurt. We only waited a few minutes but I had to keep telling myself to breathe, because I couldn't seem to remember how to do that.

Then I heard someone say, "Here they come." And the babies began to arrive, in their nannies' arms, one after the other, almost like a parade. Roger called out each child's Chinese name and then the parents' names. I was out of my chair, crossing the room.

"Where are you going?" Pat whispered. Roger hadn't called our names, but I'd noticed the second baby at the door. My baby. She was frowning just the way she was in that little picture I'd memorized. Then Roger called her name and ours and I was holding my daughter. She was the most beautiful thing I had ever seen. I couldn't take my eyes away from her. I know they'd said it wasn't possible to love her on sight but oh, I did. She was very quiet, serious. Most of the other babies cried, but Lauren didn't. She let me hold her and didn't even try to go back to the nanny. Mostly she looked puzzled. She was probably wondering, who is this crazy woman dripping tears all over me?

I had to sit down. I held Lauren on my lap and counted fingers and toes, picked through her messy hair looking for lice. (None, thank goodness.) Her clothes were small and she didn't have anything on her feet — not even socks. She was grubby. Then she coughed and took a couple of wheezy breaths. I used a tissue to wipe her nose and pretended I didn't feel the fear that had just stuck its arm down my throat and grabbed my stomach.

The nanny who had come in with Lauren sat beside me. Chen Ping spoke some English. I thanked her over and over for taking care of Lauren and tried to think of what I should ask her. She said Lauren likes music. When I asked what she ate, the nanny said milk, but I don't know if she meant real milk, soymilk or formula. And she likes bread and something that sounds like "congee."

Then she said, "I love her very much," in careful English. I could see she was trying not to cry. I hugged her. "So do I," I said.

So much of the rest is a blur. People were laughing, crying, talking, all at the same time. The room whirled around me as I held my child. I finally said to Pat, "Would you like to hold your daughter?"

"This is Daddy," I told the baby as I handed her up to him. I'd never seen his face shine with such happiness.

October 5, 1998 (Nanning)

When we started back to our room last night I felt as though I was carrying a paper-thin piece of china. My hands seemed too awkward and too small all at the same time. Pat's arms hovered around me. I think he was afraid I would drop Lauren. He was like a basketball player under the net, ready to snatch the ball.

We sat Lauren on the bed between us and just stared at her. When I took my hand away from her back, she wobbled and fell over. She's so tiny and floppy, like a rag doll.

She took a bottle. We gave her a sponge bath on the bed and put on the pink sleeper. Finally I put Lauren in the crib. I watched her and she watched me. She fell asleep first. Lauren coughed most of the night, sometimes so hard she couldn't get her breath. I rubbed her back. I rubbed her chest. She seemed to be better up, so I carried her around the room for a while and tried to make myself not be terrified, but I was. I think she could have the flu or bronchitis. It doesn't sound good but I don't want to panic.

I'm supposed to know how to do this. It's my job to take care of my daughter and I'm going to do it well. I'm going to be a good mother. She doesn't know it yet because she doesn't know me yet, but I'm not going to let her down.

At dawn, Pat called Paul Chee-a-tow. He sent Roger who was trying to help, but his main agenda for the day was to get the paperwork done. Then Louisa came with the orphanage director, one of the nannies and someone they said was a doctor from the orphanage. Let her be a real doctor, please God, I thought and was ashamed of myself for being so small-minded. The orphanage director took Lauren out of my arms. I wrapped one hand over the other and squeezed until the ends of my fingers bulged red, to keep myself from grabbing her back from the director.

Louisa translated the doctor's questions and my answers, while the doctor examined the baby. Finally the doctor handed me three twists of paper filled with powder she had mixed with a mortar and pestle, plus a tiny vial of liquid.

"Mix the powder in the liquid," Louisa translated, "Give it to the baby every four hours." What if this is wrong was all I could think, but I let the doctor give Lauren the first dose. I wish she had spoken English. I wish I spoke some Mandarin. I wish we were home.

I hope someone is in charge of all this somewhere in the universe. If anything happens to Lauren I will hurt somebody and they can leave me here forever because I won't be sorry and I won't care.

The director kept saying things to Louisa, then looking at me and shaking her head. She looked at the baby bottles I'd unpacked and I didn't need a translator to tell me she disapproved. She took them out of my hands and slit all the nipples with a razor blade. I think maybe I could work up a real dislike for her. She's an intimidating woman.

The blankets were wrong too — not heavy enough — and Lauren is supposed to be wearing two pairs of sleepers, the director explained through Louisa. Two? I glanced at the window. The air had the same hazy, heavy look as yesterday, when the heat and humidity had wrapped around us like a hot, wet wool blanket.

But it's an unknown country for me and I know I don't travel so well.

I hadn't had much sleep and I had to keep swallowing so I wouldn't cry. So all I said was *Xièxie*, thank you, the only word in Mandarin I know. The director's eyes did a slow circuit of the room. She said some things Louisa didn't translate. I wondered what else I was doing wrong. Then they left. In a few minutes Lauren's cough got a little easier and she was breathing okay. As soon as I could get my arms around her again, I felt better.

October 6, 1998 (Nanning)

At breakfast yesterday, I found out what congee is: rice gruel made with fish brine. I tried a spoonful, gagged, and swallowed only because there was nowhere to spit.

After breakfast we piled on the bus to begin the adoption paperwork process. Roger was upset about the time, because we were late. First we went to the government department that oversees adoption, signed papers and had a little ceremony. Then we went to the notary's office.

Sitting with Lauren on my lap waiting for our turn to get all the documents notarized, I felt my heart begin to race. This is just a formality, I kept saying in my head. Because already I can't give her back. I didn't think it was possible to be this happy and this terrified all at once.

I'm doing this all wrong. The clothes I brought are too warm. Lauren hates the Pablum. And the Snugli. She almost gave herself whiplash trying to twist her way out of it yesterday. She screamed when I tried to give her a bath. And she coughed most of the night again. I feel inadequate.

We saw some of Nanning this afternoon. Roger took us to a pretty little park. I was fascinated by a statue being restored — a giant teacup — surrounded by staging, all made from lengths of bamboo lashed together.

We also went to a downtown department store where I got Lauren a pair of pants, some shorts and a tee shirt. And more tissues.

Here you can't just choose something off the shelf and take it to the checkout. A clerk — they all seem to be young women — takes your purchase and gives you a piece of paper with the price, almost like a voucher. Then you go to a little kiosk and pay the cashier. She gives you a receipt to take back to the clerk who has what you bought waiting in a bag.

The people are so friendly. They smile at the baby in Pat's two-dollar stroller. Then they point to the flag on my pack and say, "Canadian?" I nod. "Lucky baby." I smile, point at myself and say, "Lucky." My cheeks hurt from smiling.

A little girl about five, clutching her father's hand, came up to me in the store. She stared at me, then Lauren, then me again. She turned to her father. I couldn't follow what she was saying, but I could hear the question in her voice. He answered and I caught the word, "Canada." She smiled and reached out a finger to Lauren who grabbed it and grinned, showing off her four teeth.

The father smiled at me and pointed at Lauren. "Pretty," he said in English.

I pointed at his little girl. "Pretty," I echoed about his daughter.

Except for the fact that I'm ten thousand miles from home we were just a couple of parents feeling proud of our kids. He tugged at the little girl's hand. She gave me a shy smile and they moved on.

That could have been Lauren, I realized. But it won't be. A path she won't take because of choices both her mothers made.

October 7, 1998 (Wuzhou)

It took about eleven hours to get here to Wuzhou by bus. More than once, I almost fell asleep sitting up. Lauren slept a couple of times and we looked out the window a lot. I even managed to change her diaper on the seat. We'll be here for a couple of days. This is where we get passports for the babies. Roger calls Wuzhou "shabby." To me it seems forgotten. The guidebook had called it a booming city!

My menstrual cycle is completely out of whack. Doing the "woman thing" on an eleven-hour bus ride — my body's turning on me. I'm glad I followed Diane McAdam's advice about bringing tampons.

They found us a better bus for the trip, a government bus with air conditioning and a sound system. And a tape of what I'm guessing is "The Carpenters' Greatest Hits." I am definitely sleep deprived; I liked it.

We stopped for a bathroom break after a couple of hours. The "bathroom" was a concrete trough in the floor, divided into four stalls by waist-high walls. I gagged at the smell before I was even inside, but I knew I wasn't going to see another bathroom for at least a couple more hours. I stuffed my roll of toilet paper under my chin and hiked up my skirt with one hand, clutching my hand sanitizer in the other. I only looked down once to see where my feet were. I kept my eyes in the far corner of the room where a fat, green-hued fly crawled up the concrete wall, and promised myself that I'd never make another gas station bathroom joke again.

We had lunch at a restaurant in a little town just off the highway. They put us in a small banquet room at the end of a long hallway, with a television and a karaoke machine. A waitress brought steaming cloths to wipe our hands and faces. The meal began with soup. Steam spiraled up from the bowl. I figured it was safe to eat. After the soup more platters of food continued to arrive. I didn't eat anything with meat or that didn't seem hot enough to sear the roof of my mouth. So much of the food is cooked with more oil than I expected. My stomach is a lot better since the surgery, but I can't put all that oil into it and expect it to stay that way. I'd rather be hungry until we get home. I haven't tried vomiting with that new valve and I'd really be happy if I didn't have to test it here.

I got directions to the bathroom from Roger. I cut through the kitchen. On one counter I caught sight of rows of pigs knuckles and oxtails. Or maybe they were water buffalo tails. All I know is at one time they were definitely waving from the backside of something.

I stood for a moment on the small balcony outside the bathroom. Wooden crates heaped with cabbage and other vegetables were piled on the stairs. Scrawny chickens scratched in cages. Below in the courtyard, rusty metal drums overflowed with garbage, the sour smell rising through the heavy air. There was laundry hanging in the windows of some of the apartments ringing the courtyard. Others had wire cages jutting out with a couple of chickens pecking inside.

It's so different. I felt very small because all I've ever known is my own little corner of the world.

I miss my corner.

October 8, 1998 (Wuzhou)

I feel helpless and tired and homesick and I want to scream at everyone. I should be wearing one of those jackets with arms that tie in the back.

I killed a couple of mosquitoes in our hotel room. The crib was too small, the sides way too low. Lauren's cough scares me and I don't care what kind of a horrible person it makes me, I don't have any faith in the doctor now.

Then Roger said the orphanage director wanted to interview each family. I slumped against the wall just inside our room and cried. The director is always looking for me so she can tell me something I'm doing wrong. She doesn't speak any English, but she always manages to get the message across. And if I do what she suggests, the next time she spots me suddenly that's wrong.

I felt dirty, hungry and exhausted. Half asleep, Lauren sagged in my arms. I don't know if it was exhaustion, but all at once I was furious, full of anger and frustration. I complained about having these interviews at a time when we are all exhausted. I raved about the crib. I became a horrible, obnoxious person. I think I'm just not meant to leave home. I get out of my yard and my worst side appears.

Pat tried to explain that all we want is the chance to put Lauren to bed and get some sleep ourselves. He's more diplomatic than I am. He's like the man with the big shovel that follows the elephants in the parade.

(Later)

In the end, we gave our donations and the gifts of clothing to the orphanage, but the interviews were postponed. A better crib arrived from somewhere. Roger came to the door with bananas and apples.

I stood in the shower and cried because I think I've antagonized almost everyone in the group and a few Chinese officials besides. I have that feeling of being in the fourth grade and no one wants to eat lunch or hang upside down from the monkey bars with me. I'm so tired, I feel sick. I'm wheezing as much as Lauren is.

When I got into bed Pat said, "You're not going to get us thrown into a communist prison, are you?" I poked him with my elbow. Hard.

(Later)

I got into the bathtub with Lauren. And Lauren didn't scream. She clutched my arm with her hand, but I got her properly bathed. And I got her to eat the Pablum too. I crushed half a Farley biscuit in with the cereal. I don't even know why I brought those biscuits. Maybe I'm not as incompetent as I think I am.

Pat has to be as scared as I am, but I never see it. The only support he gets from me is, "Are you okay?" sometime during the day. He doesn't know anything about babies, but he's learning fast. He gives Lauren her bottle and her cereal in the morning, while I get dressed. Sometimes I stand in the bathroom doorway and watch the two of them.

We lie in the dark every night, jammed into that little bed so we can both be closer to Lauren. And when she starts to cough, Pat squeezes my hand and I remember that I'm not doing this all alone.

I tried to ask the director about the orphanage and the nannies' relationships with the children. I wanted to be able to tell Lauren something about her life there, but I don't think it's something they talk about. Louisa hesitated before she asked the question. The director shook her head and made a dismissive gesture in the air. "Was that wrong?" I asked Louisa. "I didn't mean to be rude." Another question I don't have answers to.

I can't stop wondering where Lauren's other mother is. Did I pass her on the street? Did she see us go by on the bus? Louisa said that after she left Lauren for the people from the orphanage to find, she was probably hiding close by, waiting and watching. I wish there was some way to tell her that her baby is safe and loved. I'm trying to imagine her desperation and sadness, but what I feel is guilt, because her pain gave me my happiness. Already Lauren is the joy of my life. I think about giving her up and my mind refuses to go there. And secretly, I'm glad it doesn't have to.

Lauren tried to stand on her head this morning. We were playing on the floor and I stood Dolly, the little pink rag doll I brought, on her head. Lauren put her head and hands down on the floor and her skinny little backside stuck up in the air.

We went to the police station today to apply for the babies' passports. We had to walk part of the way. I've never been anywhere with so many people. They stared and I stared right back. It didn't seem to be rude the way it would have seemed at home. I didn't see anyone who didn't smile.

The whole city smells as though it's rotting. People step over garbage as though they don't even see it. Under a street sign, I saw a woman help a toddler in pongee pants squat to pee.

At the station, we waited our turn in a small, sweltering room. The officer's English was very good and his questions were easy. I realized he was picking things out of our home study. I was quiet and polite. I didn't cause any international incidents today.

October 9, 1998

I've gotten to know Susan Swanson and her daughter Jamie from Saskatchewan. Susan is adopting twins. She and her husband Morley own a farm that he just couldn't leave for two weeks, so Jamie, who's in university, took time off and came along to help. Susan told me that they asked for twins and she's overjoyed to have them because there aren't that many sets of twins available for adoption and the wait is usually longer.

Susan and Jamie talked me into going shopping with them and the twins last night. Lauren cried when I left. "Go," Pat said. "I can handle everything." I knew he could, but I got to the elevator and almost turned back. I was sure I could still hear Lauren crying even though I was too far away.

I was rubbing my eyes to keep them open, but I did want to go. I wanted Lauren to have something from the place where she was born. We wandered around the shopping center and I finally chose a string of jade beads from a little jewelry store by the main entrance. They won't be special to her for a while, but I hope that someday she'll wear them and have good thoughts about her first home. I hope we can bring her back some day.

Jamie bought a great pair of red suede shoes and bargained on the price. We walked away feeling like we got a great deal and I'm guessing from the laughing in the store behind us that the people there felt the same way.

We came back to the hotel in a pedi-cab, weaving through the darkness and laughing every time we hit a bump. We laughed a lot.

(Later)

Lauren coughs herself awake so I pick her up and walk around the room until she gets drowsy again. My eyes feel like they're lined with sandpaper. But then she smiles at me and I know that if anyone ever breaks her heart, I'll have to kill him.

The others went to the orphanage this morning. We didn't go. Lauren didn't get much sleep and I'm worried about that bus ride to Guangzhou tomorrow. (I've probably pissed off a few people again.) I wheeled Lauren around for a while in the stroller and she took a long nap. So did Pat. I did some packing and tried to get things organized. I don't know if I accomplished anything, but I like the illusion that I did.

Lauren's a flirt. She's very taken with Emma Heidrichs' daddy, Henry. Henry, Cathy and Emma are in the room next door to us. Lauren tried to climb over Emma this morning, just to get in Henry's face and smile at him. This afternoon she crawled around Jeff and Candace Wilson's room for a while with some of the other babies. It's only the second time I've had a few minutes to spend with anyone else in the group. Most of the time I was on the floor with the babies. I think everyone is tired and eager to get back to Beijing where the food is better. Jeff has been especially resourceful. He's found bread, milk and other food. He's risen to the challenge of this trip and I think I'm sinking like a cement block.

October 10, 1998 (Wuzhou)

Now when I go to the bathroom, Lauren crawls after me, sits outside the door and cries. When I come out again she gives me a look that's a mix of relief and joy, as though she'd been sitting outside the door for a month and had almost given me up for dead.

I killed another mosquito last night and then obsessively checked my arms and legs for any sign I'd been bitten. Please God, I thought. Don't let me get malaria and I won't ask you for anything else. God and I both know I'm lying. But I'm hoping, for Lauren's sake, he'll cut me a little slack.

I wish there was a better way to say thank you to Lauren's nanny. When I asked Chen Ping about her work at the orphanage she deflected my questions by talking about Lauren instead. I can see by the way she touches Lauren's hand with a gentle finger, and watches for us, smiling when she catches sight of the baby, that she loves her. I don't know how many babies she's had to say good-bye to, but it has to be wrenching every time. Lauren is special, she says. She calls her Ying-Ying. She asked if I would write and send pictures. I said yes, and nodded, so she'd know this is something I want to do. For Lauren, it will be a connection to her first home.

Chen Ping brought me her address neatly written on a bit of paper. I copied it into my notebook — just to be safe — and slipped the paper into my wallet. I won't be able to tell Lauren about her birth mother or her life in the orphanage. I can at least give her this.

This morning while we were waiting in the lobby to check out, the director wanted to pick Lauren up to say good-bye. "Ying-Ying," she said, and reached out to take the baby from me. Lauren shrank into me and grabbed my shirt. I shook my head and wrapped both arms tightly around my baby.

Deep inside, no matter what Pat said, I was terrified Lauren wouldn't like me. Everything I'd read warned that it's harder for a child over a year old to bond. So I was prepared for her to cry, to scream, to push me away. But somehow she seems to know that I'm her mother.

She has decided she can be out of my sight if Pat is pushing her in the stroller. Every night after her bath they go for a tour of the hallway. And there's always at least one other dad doing the same thing. Sometimes I look down the hall and Pat's bent over the stroller talking and Lauren is looking up, listening intently. I think they're either plotting to overthrow the government or scheming to ditch me and make a break for the nearest McDonalds.

October 11, 1998 (Beijing)

I've been a mother for a whole week now. Next Sunday, we'll be home. I'll be able to wash the bottles in the sink and brush my teeth from the tap and shave my legs. And sleep. Lack of sleep has eroded most of my good qualities.

The bus trip to Guangzhou was easy — less than six hours. The Gitic River is a very nice hotel. Our room was a little bigger than the last two. At the gift shop in the lobby, I bought Lauren a Chinese tea set with panda bears.

We had spaghetti for supper. I wanted to stuff my face in the plate when it came. I was so happy to eat something that hadn't been fried. And the breakfast buffet was glorious. I walked around three times just to look. Real juice. Chilled yogurt in sealed containers. Plain bread. And a lot of other things. I drank three glasses of juice.

We were up very early — at five. At least Lauren didn't cough as much last night. I gave her some Dimetapp before we left the hotel and I put decongestant drops in her nose just before our flight took off for Beijing. (Pissed her off a bit, but she didn't have any problems taking off or landing.)

Dave and Theresa Orlando are sick. I don't know if it's something they ate or the flu. Theresa's too sick to take care of little Elizabeth. I watched her at the airport. She looked as though it was taking all her effort to stand up. So I offered to take Elizabeth. We had her with us from lunchtime until tonight, just a little while ago. It was fun. Lauren was jealous. She sat on my lap — with Elizabeth — for the first time. If I picked Elizabeth up, no matter what Lauren was doing, she wanted to be picked up too.

Elizabeth is a sweet baby. She wouldn't let Pat hold her, but she seemed to like me. Babies, cats and old people always like me. It's everyone else I have problems with.

October 12, 1998(Beijing)

My chest hurts to breathe and I cough when I lie down. I think whatever Lauren has I now have too. I miss everything and everyone at home. I miss hearing a language all around me that I can understand. I miss the clear, sharpness of the air. I want to go home.

It's as though Canada doesn't exist here. We found a little American news on CNN. Quebec could be a separate country now, or Brian Tobin could have taken Newfoundland and joined Iceland, and I'd never know about it.

October 13, 1998 (Beijing)

When the housekeeping staff cleans the room, they leave a thermos jug of boiling water. I use it all by mid-afternoon. Sunday, I left Pat watching Elizabeth and Lauren sleep and went to look for more hot water. I'd looked up the word for water in my Lonely Planet guidebook — *kāi shuǐ*. In the hall, I met one of the young men who works in housekeeping. He pointed at my jug. "Hot water?" he asked.

I nodded. He took the container, gestured that I should wait and disappeared around the corner. I hoped he wouldn't come back with a thermos of tea.

He returned in a moment, the jug filled with steaming water, and I thanked him. (I don't think I'm pronouncing "thank you" properly in Mandarin. Everyone giggles when I say it.) Now, I think he watches for me. He appears before I get a dozen steps down the hall. Yesterday I was on another floor when his head popped out an open doorway. "Hot water, hello," he said. "Hello," I said, and we grinned at each other as though we were great friends.

October 14, 1998 (Beijing)

After I get up in the night to check on Lauren, I look at my watch. Then when I get back into bed, I try to figure out what everyone is doing at home. Home is twelve hours behind here. I like to picture everybody doing their day, just the way I'd be if I were home. It makes me feel not so far away.

We went to the Lufthansa Center, a multi-story shopping center that I think is named after the German airline. I bought Lauren a rattle, a blue and yellow hard plastic dog, which plays "Somewhere Over The Rainbow." She loves it. She points. I push the button. It plays, over and over again. I tried to entice her to choose a little terry cloth bear rattle. But she's determined when she has made up her mind.

I bought myself an embroidered satin vest and for Lauren a pair of pink silk Chinese pajamas.

We walked to Carrefors, the grocery store, this afternoon to get water and arrowroot cookies to last until Friday. I almost bought Lauren a jacket.

She kept patting it. It was fuzzy fake fur fabric with white teddy bears on a salmon-colored background.

We went for Lauren's medical examination at suppertime. Before we were called in, I whispered to her, "Please be an angel baby for me." A lot of the other babies had cried. Not her. She was too busy flirting with the doctor. Pat was all charm with the nurse who weighed and measured Lauren. She was a blonde Scandinavian goddess and very nice. There was no one left for me to flirt with.

The doctor prescribed an iron supplement. He said Lauren is very small for her age. But he thinks her age is accurate. Most important, she's healthy enough to travel and we're going home in a couple of days.

October 15, 1998 (China)

I love to watch Lauren sleep. I think about all she's going to do in the future and all she's going to be and I wish I could protect her from all the bad parts. I know that she trusts me already. She looks for me when I leave the room. The past few mornings, she's been waking up and peeking out of the crib, and when she sees me she smiles. And I see all her trust in those smiles.

I rock slightly all the time. I see the other women do it, too. Our beautiful daughters on our hips, we sway to some melody only mothers can hear.

Less than twelve hours and we'll be starting for home. (Actually about ten hours and thirty-five minutes.) One suitcase is packed and closed. I have a few things to throw in the other in the morning, but otherwise it's mostly packed too.

We jammed the stroller into its bag and taped all the holes with duct tape we got from Jeff Wilson. I really want that stroller to make it home. It's a family heirloom now.

We took a picture at breakfast this morning of Lauren with Danny who's been our waitress in the coffee shop. She always pays special attention to Lauren. And if it's not too busy, she walks Lauren around while I eat my lunch. She sings and Lauren always smiles.

October 16, 1999 (in the air)

We're going home. We left the hotel early, because we had to stop at the embassy for the babies' visas. As usual the luggage came to the airport separately and very, very slowly. I had this image in my head of the bellboys walking it to the airport, loaded down like Sherpa guides.

We waited just inside the main doors. Bags and babies and people sitting on the floor — it was like our own little village. I had to change Lauren on the floor of the terminal — not the cleanest spot in the world but better than the bathroom.

The luggage finally came and we pushed into a line to check it and into another to hand over our departure slips. Crushed among all those people, I couldn't make out English from Mandarin. It was just a garble of noise. There were so many people pressed into the check-in area I couldn't tell if I was in the right line — or in a line at all. I kept moving forward with the luggage cart like a tank. It wasn't the place for courtesy. It was hot and close and I wanted to be taller with sharper elbows.

When I finally got to the door to the plane, I looked back and whispered, "Thank you for my baby."

(Later)

It looked gray and cold out the window of the plane as we descended into Vancouver. But to me it was beautiful. I had the urge to kiss the pilots and sing "O Canada." I would have kissed the pavement if I could have actually gotten down to it. Even though home is on the other coast I felt a rush of happiness.

As soon as we were off the plane Lauren and I were striding through the airport at my top walking speed toward Immigration. Pat is tall and he has long legs, so I figured he'd find a way to keep up. We were probably the fifth or sixth couple through. Lauren is now officially a landed immigrant. And she's been changed on the floor of both the Beijing and the Vancouver airports.

(Montréal)

I think I've been up now for about twenty-eight hours. It's tomorrow in Beijing. But it's still today here and my head feels like a balloon that's had way too much air blown into it.

They lost our luggage. The customer service rep was rude. I lost my temper. And I don't care what the little pissant thought. I told him I was going to call my lawyer.

At least the hotel is nice. And the staff. When they found out about our lost luggage, they brought us robes and a curling iron for me. They promised to call if the luggage showed up, no matter what time it is.

I was crying in the bathroom a while ago, trying to wash Lauren's dirty sleepers. I felt like a rotten mother because I am so shallow that I wanted her to be all dressed up when we got home. I was stewing in self-pity when Rhonda called. I don't think she knows how much she helped. It was wonderful to hear her familiar voice. I think the logical, sensible, nice part of me got lost on the way to Wuzhou.

Lauren is asleep. By some blessing we made it. I didn't do it well, but I did do it. And home is almost close enough to touch.

Stage Five:
LIFE WITH YOUR CHILD

When you get home with your child, you'll experience "real life." In the first few weeks, you'll learn more about your little one. You'll establish routines and family rituals such as reading a favorite book every night before bed or kissing all the stuffed toys good morning. If this is your first child, you'll get used to the idea of being someone's parent. You'll begin to relax.

CREATING A FAMILY

During your first months together, your child will learn to trust you and to feel secure in her new family. She'll see that when you go out, you come back again, just as you told her you would. She'll learn that you do what you said you would do, whether it's giving her a drink or taking away a toy when she misbehaves. She'll discover that you come to her every time she's hurt, every time she's scared, every time she feels insecure. She'll find that she can lose her temper and still your love doesn't disappear.

For the first couple of weeks after we returned home, we cocooned in the house and restricted visitors. Talking to other adoptive parents, I've discovered many other families did the same. This time alone together can help everyone begin to feel like a family. It's a chance to set a routine and get comfortable with it, a chance to relax and have fun.

Once home, some parents continue the routine their child followed in the orphanage, as much as they can. For example, they continue with the same number of naps. They try to offer familiar foods at each meal. That's something we did.

From the beginning, Lauren slept in her own room in her crib without any problem, although I learned never to tuck in the ends of her blankets. She'd just keep pulling until everything was loose. Other parents believe strongly in the concept of the "family bed" to help them bond. Their child may sleep with them for a few months to a year or longer. Choose whichever feels right for you and your child.

There's a lot to learn in the first weeks about your child's likes and dislikes. I discovered Lauren hated bananas. They were the only food I offered in the first two weeks home that she refused.

Keep in mind that children who aren't accustomed to a lot of food may be overwhelmed at first by the abundance in North America. One mother said the first time she took her daughter inside a grocery store, the child looked around in awe and then sat on the floor and burst into tears. Some children, like my own daughter, will insist for a while on holding a bit of food in each hand as they eat. Others will eat past the point that they've had enough, until they learn that there will be plenty of food again later. If it helps, show your child that there is more applesauce in the bowl or more Cheerios in the box for another time. Reassure him that there will be more food when he's hungry again. And ask your family doctor for guidance.

In your first weeks as a family, you'll not only discover what your baby likes to eat, you'll find out what activities she enjoys. Does she want the swing to go fast or does she refuse to get in it at all? Will she go for a walk in the stroller or will she try to climb out of it before you're at the bottom of the driveway? Does she like to try new things or sit on the sidelines and watch? Take your cue from your child. Introduce new activities, new people, new toys slowly. Her entire world has changed and that can be daunting for many children.

Keep in mind there still may be more paperwork for you. Adoption officials in your child's birth country may require one or more assessments by your social worker during your child's first year with you. Check with your facilitator for specifics. At the same time ask if they provide any after-adoption programs. Some agencies offer playgroups, culture camp, language lessons and more.

THE OUTSIDE WORLD

You're happy and proud of your child and want her to meet everyone you love. And there are a lot of people waiting to meet the newest member of your family. Your baby can quickly end up with a social calendar that rivals a celebrity's. Again follow your child's lead. Some children are friendly and social and aren't afraid of new things. Others are shy or still grieving for their past caregivers. Start slowly and see what happens. Don't insist your child be picked up or held. Some children aren't ready for that kind of closeness with new people.

You may find yourself becoming an "ambassador" for adoption. Several times I've been approached by someone who asks, in an apologetic voice, "Excuse me, but is she adopted?" As long as I'm not in the middle of a meal or struggling with the wagon, a loaded backpack and too many library books, I don't mind answering the query. "Why do you ask?" I usually say. And the next question is, "Could you tell me how you did it?"

HONORING YOUR CHILD'S HERITAGE

When children are adopted as babies there's no way to know how much from their first months' experiences stays with them. There's no way to know what they miss from that time. Eventually your child may want a connection with her birth country. She may have a need to know more about her background and her birth parents. Honoring your child's culture and teaching her about the country where she was born while she's still small is a way to maintain a tie to your child's heritage, a link she may follow later if that's what she chooses. I want my daughter to have respect and pride for her Chinese heritage. I want to give her all the knowledge I can and let her choose what has meaning for her.

Look for books and videos about your child's birth country. Check at your library for music. Contact the multicultural association, if there is one where you live, for information on groups and celebrations special to your child's homeland. If there are other adoptive parents with children from the same country, try to get together several times a year and celebrate together. Incorporate traditions and celebrations into your family life. We now celebrate our own "Adoption Day," the day we legally became a family, and the Chinese New Year. Invite your family and friends to participate. Lauren's playschool class celebrated the Chinese New Year. The children learned about China, practiced saying "Gong Xi Fa Cai" — Happy New Year — and had a special snack that included pieces of orange for a sweet life.

AS YOUR CHILD GROWS

As soon as you get home, remember to apply for citizenship for your child. Be sure to specify that you need an application package for a child. It may take several months for your application to be processed and there is a fee.

For me, it was important that Lauren become a citizen as soon as possible. I wanted her to have the protection and respect being a Canadian conveys. And I hope she's proud to be part of her adopted country.

When I look at my child she doesn't look Asian to me. She just looks like my daughter. At this point in time, we haven't had any difficult experiences as a multicultural family. On a day-by-day basis, it's not something I even think about. So far our little corner of the world has been very safe, filled with people who've been happy to welcome Lauren. As her world gets bigger, it may not stay this safe. It seems unrealistic to think she won't have to deal with prejudice at some point in her life. In any case, we want Lauren to be capable of dealing with whatever comes her way. The following are some strategies that we hope will stand her in good stead, regardless of what she has to confront in the future. Do what feels right for your family and develop your own strategies.

Teach your child to think about other people's feelings. A child who is caring and compassionate toward others is less likely to be prejudiced herself.

Encourage respect for other cultures. Give your child the chance to know a variety of people — different ethnicities, different ages, different religions.

Fight ignorance with knowledge. Invite your child's friends to celebrate a special event in her culture, such as Kwanzaa or the Chinese New Year.

Teach your child that discrimination is wrong. Insist that no one is teased, left out or picked on because of the way they look or speak, or because of their gender, religion or a disability.

Point out prejudice when you see it in books, movies and television shows. Encourage your child to think about why it's wrong. Give her your support if she challenges biased attitudes. Help her come up with specific things to say when she's the victim of prejudice.

Help your child feel confident and proud. Show your appreciation for the things that make your child special. Applaud her efforts.

Be a good example. Hold yourself to the same standards to which you hold your child. Speak up when someone makes a racist remark or tells a bigoted joke. You don't have to be confrontational. A simple "please don't talk like that around us," usually works.

I'm teaching my child to be proud of who she is. I'm teaching her how to answer back to ignorance. I'm teaching her that the problem isn't hers, that she's smart, strong, beautiful, talented and very loved. I'm teaching her that her Chinese heritage is something to be celebrated, the same way we celebrate being Canadian. And I'm trying to be a good example. I'm trying to confront my own biases and learning to speak up, even when the ignorance isn't directed at us.

I don't know if this will be enough. But as long as Lauren grows up proud of who she is, I believe she'll be able to deal with the rest of the world.

Journal

October 17, 1998

HOME.

The luggage showed up at the hotel at about one a.m. Clean clothes. I even found my lipstick.

Lauren was the only child on the flight home to Fredericton. The flight attendant came into the terminal to get us to pre-board and the captain came out to welcome us once we were on the plane. As we settled into our seats, I had the sense that this is probably a bit what it's like to travel with Julia Roberts.

The world was so sharp, so clean and clear in the sunshine as the plane descended. Everyone was waiting at the airport — Pat's mother and father, my mum, and Rhonda, Bob and Laura. It was everything I wanted Lauren's coming home to be.

Pearl had painted a "welcome home" poster for us. Balloons were flying from the railing on the stairs, compliments of the grandmothers. Inside the house there was lots of food, a stack of mail and a pile of presents.

One of the gifts was a floppy, soft teddy bear with a slightly puzzled expression. We named him Bill, after Bill Dunnett, who sent him. Lauren keeps crawling over and patting Bill, the bear, so I think she likes him.

I carried her around, letting her peek into every room and stare at everything. I kept saying, "This is home." I know the words don't mean anything to her, but I hope she can feel how happy I am to be home with her.

I wanted to touch everything in the house myself. When no one was looking, I drank from the bathroom tap.

October 18, 1998

Lauren turns at the sound of her name. Already she knows what those sounds mean. She's so beautiful. Her hair is dark brown and her skin is fair and creamy, like silk to touch. She has big eyes, so dark brown they're almost black.

Pat confessed today that he had wanted Lauren to be pretty. I wanted her to be smart. It lasts longer.

October 19, 1998

I think the honeymoon is over. That easy-going, even-tempered baby disappeared while I was cooking supper and the mother ship beamed down a foul, crabby little person who wanted to be carried everywhere *right now*.

She sat in the middle of the kitchen floor and screamed, her face red and blotchy and her small fists clenched. I tried to explain that I had to get supper, but I don't think babies care about logic — especially in a language they don't understand.

While she was screeching, I suddenly realized that I'm the mommy. I didn't feel fear or panic. It was mostly a sense of confusion. *How did this happen?* I know that's kind of strange since I've been trying to make this happen for almost two years and I've just spent two weeks in a communist country ten thousand miles away, pissing off pretty much everyone I met. Mostly what hit me was the realization that I have actually managed to pull this off.

October 22, 1998

Karen Reid-Leblanc came to interview us for *Information Morning* on CBC. She asked me why we had chosen international adoption, but most of her questions were about our trip to China.

I still have whatever exotic virus I caught from the baby. My voice has a raspy quality that doesn't sound like me at all. Lauren is still coughing and when she isn't, I'm lying in bed anticipating. I am so deprived of sleep that I'm beginning to get a little buzzed — kind of the feeling I get from an occasional glass of wine.

We took Lauren for a complete check-up today. I gave Dr. Ramsey the paperwork they'd given me at the clinic in Beijing. She says we need to start from scratch on the baby's immunizations. She wants to test Lauren for HIV and hepatitis and do other blood tests as well. And Lauren does have an ear infection. This is my first diagnosis as a mother. It was work not being smug.

The doctor finished examining Lauren and suddenly turned to me and said, "You sound awful. Let me listen to your chest."

I have bronchitis.

October 23, 1998

We listened to the CBC interview while we ate breakfast. All day people have been calling, saying they heard us on the radio. I've been on the radio for years, but add some Lauren-babble and suddenly people are impressed.

Tonight Lauren sat in the tub seat without me behind her for moral support and she didn't mind at all. I was a wreck. I kept one hand on the seat and the other on her back. I was holding on so tightly my fingers cramped. She laughed and played with her rubber duck. She even splashed me once, and I could tell she was thinking, *c'mon ma, loosen up.*

If she's having problems with all the changes in her life, I can't see them. She eats everything except bananas. She sleeps all night and takes two naps.

I keep hearing, "Wait until she starts walking. Wait until she's teething." Already I can pick out the parents whose kid cried for a week with every new tooth or whose little darling toilet-papered the living room as soon as he could manage more than five steps. They always say, "Just wait," whenever I say how easy Lauren is. Then their eyes narrow and they give me a gleeful grin and I can tell they're getting some kind of endorphin rush just thinking about it.

October 27, 1998

Lauren cried as the lab technician took blood. I wanted to grab her and run. Instead I held her down and tried not to cry myself as my heart pounded. Nobody told me being a mother would make me feel so vulnerable.

The x-ray was easier. The technician put Lauren in this contraption that kept her arms over her head and I put on the lead apron and held her hands. She looked completely perplexed, but she didn't make a sound.

I've noticed Lauren watches my mouth when I talk, frowning a little and looking very much like that first little picture. Sometimes when she's babbling at me from her high chair, I wonder if it's Chinese she's speaking and if she's wondering why I don't answer.

Pat is already "Da." I'm "Bubba." I wonder what the Chinese word for mother is. I point to myself and say, "Mama." Lauren laughs and says, "Bubba," and sometimes I think I'm the butt of some baby joke.

October 28, 1998

We saw the pediatrician today. I liked him. How could you not like a doctor who sits down on the floor in his sock feet and plays with your kid?

He said Lauren has bonded really well with me and I just sat there with my big gooney grin — like I hadn't worried about it for the last year or so. Our bond is strong and deep and I couldn't love Lauren any more. Not even if I'd created her in love and sheltered her for nine months with my body. I don't know how it happened and I've given up trying to explain our connection to anyone.

There's a Chinese folktale that says soul mates are destined to be together. They are already bound to each other by an invisible red thread. Maybe it works that way for mothers and children too.

I always thought no matter how bad things got I could handle them. Okay, probably not very well, but I really believed I could make it through to the other side of anything. Now I see that's all blown to hell, because if anything happened to her I would stop living too. I would sit in a corner until I was nothing but a pile of dust and bones. Now my prayers are simple: *Put it all on me, Big Guy, just leave her out of it. Amen.*

October 29, 1998

Kicked the eye doctor, right in the diaphragm. I was holding Lauren's arms while he put drops in her eyes and I told him she'd kick. When she did, I must have looked as though I had some kind of twitch, as I tried not to laugh.

I'm trying to help Lauren get stronger, so we sit on the floor feet to feet and she tries to push me over. Every so often, I roll over sideways with grunts and funny faces and she laughs so hard sometimes she tips over herself. No one has ever thought I'm as funny as Lauren thinks I am.

November 2, 1998

Lauren likes to heckle the runners when I take her out in the stroller. She hangs over the side and blows raspberries at them as they go by. I didn't teach her that. I swear.

We went to the Browns' for dinner tonight to celebrate Bob's birthday. I like being a family. I am so taken up with Lauren these days, sometimes I have to remind myself that the rest of the world is out there.

November 9, 1998

She can walk by herself.

She was holding on to the leg of my desk and she wanted to come to me. She just let go and walked four steps. And then I could see her realize what she was doing. (It's how I've always imagined walking a tightrope would be — easy until you actually think about where you are.) The look on her face was a cross between amazement and panic. I caught her before she fell. She lifted her head and gave me a big, triumphant grin. And I gave it right back to her.

November 11, 1998

Cheerios are one of Lauren's favorite foods. There are stray ones in every room of the house — on the sofa, in the bottom of the laundry basket, inside the kitchen cupboards, on top of the extra toilet paper. So I've turned into the Cheerio vacuum. I'm scrambling around after her scooping up all the lonely-onlys she leaves behind and I end up eating them because I'm usually miles from a garbage can.

She walked again today. Seven steps. I held my arms out and she had that should-I-do-it look, but I didn't have to coax her much. She gave me a huge grin and fell into my arms laughing. If sunlight sparkling across the water had a sound, it would be just like her laughter.

Some people call beginning an adoption a leap of faith. I call it jumping off the roof. To me, jumping off the roof is recognizing that what you're about to do is going to be painful, but leaping over the edge anyway, because maybe this time you'll be able to fly. Not like a leap of faith, which always seems to me to be a blind belief that somehow it will all work out when you're not even wearing your paper wings.

November 17, 1998

The only reason I have any social life at all is because Lauren does. It seems everyone wants to see her. I'm trying to balance that with eating time, sleeping time and knocking-all-the-blocks-down time.

She's already met some of our friends, some of the relatives and some of the people who coaxed me down off the roof on the dark days in the past.

We've been home for a month now. I finally feel as though I can stop holding my breath. I kept waiting for something to go wrong, for Lauren to stop eating, or not sleep, or cry all the time. And none of that happened.

In the morning, she smiles when I go in to her crib. She's even starting to hug me back. She laughs a lot. I can see that she's happy. Even though I'm not always sure I'm doing a good job, she seems to think so.

November 20, 1998

Lauren had her first two shots today. She started to cry with the second needle, and I felt like I was betraying her by holding her still.

She fell asleep eating lunch and slept for almost two hours. When she woke up she was fine, babbling and racing around. All at once she sat down, held her arms up to me and started to cry. After that, all she wanted was to sit on my lap or be carried. And she wouldn't go to Pat at all. I had to sit her on my lap so I could pee, because she howled so loud when I just started to hand her over to him. She slept cuddled up with me for close to another hour. Then she seemed to get a lot of her energy back.

She bounces back better than I do from things. I like everyone to do things my way. I like everything to happen according to my schedule. But she rolls with things in a way I never have.

People keep saying how beautiful she is. People I don't even know. If Lauren keeps hearing it so often, I'm afraid she'll think all these compliments are her due.

November 27, 1998

Having a pee by myself is a rare, exotic experience now, unless I'm staggering down the hall in the dark at two a.m. Lauren loves to come into the bathroom with me and poke my thighs. Some of the baby books say I should let her do this — the coming in, not the poking — because it will help put her in the right frame of mind when it's time to start toilet training. I'm hoping it will make her a lot more tolerant toward her own thighs than I've been toward mine.

I put some Shreddies on the tray of Lauren's high chair this morning and she gave me her sideways what-the-heck-do-you-expect-me-to-do-with-these look. I thought they might be better than Cheerios for her to practice picking up. She still hasn't really gotten the hang of the index-finger-to-thumb motion. She managed to slip a few up into her mouth, but she had more fun flicking them from side to side on the tray.

The doctor says, "Don't worry. She'll catch up."

Don't worry? I'm someone's mother. For the rest of my life, I'm never going to have a day when I don't worry.

December 1, 1998

I couldn't stop thinking about what Christmas was like for Lauren last year. Maybe it's because her first picture was taken in December.

I don't even know if they celebrate Christmas in Wuzhou. But I just couldn't stand thinking about the children still there. So I put together a parcel and sent it to the orphanage. I sent clothes of different sizes. Plus some socks and undershirts, and a few toys. I put a Christmas card on top that said it was from Ying-Ying.

It's important to me to keep the tie with Chen Ping. I can't let Lauren's birth mother know she's all right and happy, but at least someone else who cares about her knows.

Maybe some day the political situation will change in China. If Lauren's birth mother wants to find out about our daughter I want the answers to be waiting.

And I have this fantasy that Chen Ping knows something, maybe knows where Lauren came from, knows who gave birth to her. Maybe her other mother already knows Lauren is happy and very loved. I know that's not really possible. Lauren's birth mother couldn't have taken her to the orphanage. She would have been punished for abandoning her baby.

December 2, 1998

Pat and I have new wills and powers of attorney. Everything is in place legally to take care of Lauren, if something happens to us while she's still little. We've made Rhonda and Bob her guardians. I know I can trust them.

When Karen, our lawyer, brought the wills to be signed, she gave Lauren one of her business cards and told her to call, if we gave her any trouble. Lauren took it, studied it with that little serious frown she gets that wrinkles the bridge of her nose, and even ran her finger over the lettering. Just what I need: a fifteen-month-old with attitude.

Then something wonderful happened. The kind of wonderful that gives me a lump in my throat. When Karen came back with the notarized copies of the wills, she brought a big bag of presents. It was so unexpected, but just the kind of thing she does. There were chocolate Santas and animal crackers, an Eeyore hand puppet and a xylophone.

The xylophone is a big, loud hit. Lauren likes to bang on the keys and then turn it over and scrape her fingers over the ribbed back. It sounds like she's playing a washboard. Everything was wrapped in tissue paper which she adores. She crinkled paper in between gigs on the xylophone.

December 4, 1998

My head feels as though it's been packed with sand. Lauren had nightmares last night. I got up at midnight. And one-thirty. And three. And five. She couldn't seem to get out of them.

The first time she cried, I was moving before I knew I was up. She was on her hands and knees in the middle of the crib shaking. I picked her up and held her against me. Her eyes were squeezed shut so tightly I wasn't sure she was awake. I kept talking softly, rocking back and forth and finally she looked at me. And she seemed to understand that she was safe.

I wonder if these are the night terrors we were warned about. What did she dream about? What was happening in her head? My mind starts going down alleys it's not supposed to.

I don't like to say that Lauren was abandoned because I don't think she truly was. Although her mother couldn't take Lauren to the orphanage, she set the baby down where Lauren would be safe, where she knew someone from the orphanage would find a child. She was meant to have this chance. If I can't tell her anything else when she asks the hard questions I can tell her how much she has always been loved by both her mothers.

I wish there was some way I could let Lauren's other mother know she's all right.

December 17, 1998

I've been working on an article about our trip to China, mostly at night while Lauren's sleeping. After lunch, I put her in the stroller and we walked to the post office and sent it to *The New Brunswick Reader*.

Maybe it will help someone who's longing for a child and doesn't know what to do.

December 19, 1999

I have so many kids' clothes, I don't think I'll need to buy any until Lauren's in school. One of the nurses Rhonda works with has sent us a heap of clothes her children are too big to wear.

Having so much makes me feel blessed — especially so close to Christmas. So I sorted out a big pile to wash and press for the Salvation Army. Blessings keep appearing, whether I deserve them or not. I may be wrong, but I feel the world has gotten nicer since Lauren arrived here.

December 20, 1998

We set up the Christmas tree and put on the lights this morning. When Lauren got up she zoomed right over to it and walked all around as though she was checking it out from every angle.

After lunch we put on the rest of the decorations and sang along with the radio. I didn't unpack my best green and purple glass balls, but I got out everything else — the crocheted snowflakes, the little icicles I got in Florida on our honeymoon. I even hung the last two unbreakable Christmas ornaments my dad bought for my first Christmas. Lauren carried things to the tree and danced in the center of the room. I thought, this is what family feels like.

She loves music. Did that come from her mother or her father? Or did it come encoded in her DNA from generations back? Was it something she learned at the orphanage? I wonder if all the things she might never know about her background are going to trouble her someday?

I know there are going to be questions — easy ones, difficult ones, embarrassing ones. Ones I can't answer.

"At least you don't have to worry about her mother showing up on your doorstep," someone said to me. I wish that were a possibility. It would be the easy way out, a convenient source of answers to all those unanswerable questions.

December 21, 1998

Some days I truly think I need a character transplant to be a good role model. How can I teach Lauren to be a good person, when sometimes I am very small and not always sorry about it?

Today as we went into the grocery store I gave her a two-dollar coin and she put it in the Salvation Army basket. She didn't understand why we were doing it, but the lady smiled at us and said, "Merry Christmas." We smiled and said it back and everyone felt good.

December 24, 1998

On Christmas Eve, you're supposed to be able to ask for your heart's desire, at least according to a legend I read. And the angels will grant your wish.

I don't know if there really are angels. But I know if ever there was the possibility of an angel touching your life with a miracle, then what better time for it to begin than on Christmas Eve.

Last Christmas Eve, I wished for Lauren.

December 25, 1998

Lauren was fascinated by all the gifts under the tree. She didn't want to tear any wrapping paper. She wanted to carefully peel it all off and save it. Pat shook his head and laughed. "I should've expected this," he said. "She's just like you."

Mum got Lauren a little ride-on car. The trunk already has a couple of spoons, a rattle, some blocks and Pat's comb. Pat and I took turns pushing her up and down the hall until the muscles in the backs of our legs gave out. I used one of my scarves to tie her on and explained that was her seatbelt.

We couldn't get Lauren to eat anything at dinner. She just sat in her high chair beaming at each of her grandparents in turn. After everyone left, we sat by the tree with just the Christmas lights on and ate a big bowl of Cheerios.

This has been the best Christmas. Every year now I'll say that and it'll always be true. I know Lauren didn't really understand what was going on. And I know she won't remember. But I will.

December 29, 1998

We were at the drugstore a couple of days ago and, while we waited for my prescription, I talked to an elegant older woman who couldn't take her eyes off Lauren. "Do you have any grandchildren?" I asked. She shook her head. "I didn't have any children. I don't have anyone," she said. "I wish ..." She let out a breath and smiled at the baby. Then she looked at me. "Enjoy her," she said. "I do," I said, and I kissed the top of Lauren's head.

I watched her walk to her car and had the sensation that I'd just seen myself thirty years in the future of another life. Without my baby.

December 30, 1998

She decided she wasn't going to eat peas today at lunch. She smushed her little lips together and stuck out her chin just daring me to make her. I mixed the peas with supper and she ate them and didn't even notice the difference.

I always win. Me and Wonder Woman. It's the bra.

My sister, Maureen, and my niece, Karen, are here. Lauren already adores Karen. Karen can push that little car for a very long time and her legs never get wobbly. She's eighteen and full of energy. Maureen read every book Lauren dragged over to her. Last night after dinner we all sat on the couch, surrounding my mother, and Pat took our picture.

Three generations. All the women of my family.

January 3, 1999

Lauren's such a show-off. I indulge her because I don't think she ever had the chance to be anyone's shining star in the orphanage. If she turns out to be a brat, I'll spring for therapy.

Now that I'm a mother, other women with children talk differently to me. Before, I suspect no matter what I said, they weren't sure I liked children because I didn't have any.

Now it's as though I've joined a secret society. Instead of a password we talk about teething and toilet training.

January 4, 1999

My kid's a Canadian. I sent in the paperwork back in November. Citizenship Canada said it would take about ten months. But there it was today in the mail, the citizenship card and a fancy piece of paper with congratulations. The card is for identification — like a birth certificate. She's fourteen months old in the picture. I can't wait until she tries to get into a bar at twenty-one with this ID.

I'm disappointed there isn't any ceremony. I wanted that for her. Okay, for me. I wanted to hold up her little hand and take an oath. I wanted somebody in robes with lots of flags and a cake.

I haven't always been a patriotic person. But since Tiananmen Square I've come to understand, where I didn't know before, the loyalty and pride some people have for this country and its flag. The flag was just a symbol for me before, a representative, an easy way to say Canadian. Now when I see the flag it stands for all the benefits and privileges of being Canadian. I have the freedom to make choices, to express my opinions — even the bizarre ones. I have the opportunity to live peacefully and to do and be whatever I choose — even if what I choose isn't always a good decision.

And now Lauren is a Canadian and all of those choices and opportunities are hers, too.

January 5, 1999

Mark Tunney, the editor of *The New Brunswick Reader*, called at suppertime to say they want the story. They want it to run this weekend. He said my writing was good. He said a lot of other things — but I didn't hear anything after "the writing's good." It was just a jumble of sounds after that.

I danced around the living room and Lauren laughed and waved her arms. We celebrated by opening the box of chocolates someone had given us for Christmas.

The Telegraph's Fredericton photographer, Noel Chenier, is coming tomorrow to take some pictures to go with the story. It's the only other thing I remember Mark saying.

Published. Our story. My name. Big letters.

January 8, 1999

I went out for lunch today with Heather and left Lauren with Pat. And felt guilty for not being home. I think it's another of my "control freak" things. Secretly I believe that if I'm not there, the electricity will go off, the pipes will freeze and when I get home there will be eight inches of ice in the basement. And Lauren will be shivering in the middle of the living room floor in just a diaper and an undershirt. Then I felt guilty for feeling that way, as though Pat wasn't great at taking care of his own kid. I tried taking plenty of deep breaths, the way I'd been taught in the hospital after my stomach surgery.

I put my hand in my pocket, while Heather and I were talking, waiting for the food. There were three Cheerios at the bottom with the lint. And then, all I wanted was to be home.

January 9, 1999

At seven-thirty I was at the store buying six newspapers. The guy at the counter said, "Why six papers?" I turned one around and pointed to the picture on the top of page one and said, "That's my daughter." It was Lauren looming up into the camera from her crib.

There was lots of snow outside, but I ran all the way home, big loping strides as though I was running in slow motion.

Pat, Lauren and I each had a paper. I scanned to see what changes they'd made. Very few. Pat read, stopping every few paragraphs to laugh and say, "Oh Lord, I remember that." Lauren studied the pictures intently as though she was trying to decide if Noel had gotten her best side. I keep picking up the paper and grinning at Lauren on the front page above the paper's name. I have that feeling like I've been spinning around and around, giddy, out of breath and exhilarated. I like it.

We tried swimming class this afternoon. Too cold. I think we're hot tub people. I'm thinking big glasses of tropical fruit juice, lots of bubbling water and someone cute with lots of muscles to hold our towels. Oh yeah, I'm giddy.

January 14, 1999

Every day she masters something new and I am staggered by my kid's ability to learn. I'm beginning to think that Nobel Prize thing is not necessarily a fantasy.

Lauren now weighs sixteen pounds, four ounces. You would think she'd weigh more, the way she eats, but she puts out so much energy I'm sure she's burning up most of those calories. I hung right over the nurse's shoulder while she weighed Lauren to be sure the nurse did it right.

When I became Lauren's mother, she already had four teeth. She could crawl, wobbily. She'd eaten bread, bananas and rice. If the orphanage director is to be believed, she might have spent three months with her birth mother. (And on this I want to believe her.) Another nine months were spent in the orphanage. There are twelve months of my baby's life I can tell her almost nothing about.

I want to take her back to China when she's old enough to ask her own questions. I want to go back myself. I want to see the country again. I want another chance to appreciate it.

January 20, 1999

Lauren was in a kissing mood tonight. Pat's in Moncton so she has me all to herself and she really likes that. She kept running over to kiss me and when I'd stick my cheek out she'd put her little hand on my face and push it so she could kiss me on the lips. She gives big, open-mouth fish kisses and I love them.

January 23, 1999

Our story in *The Reader* provoked two pages of letters. I'm not sure that anyone else's writing has prompted such a response.

Some of the other adoptive parents didn't seem to like what I wrote. Their stories about their China experiences all seem to be a little more "glowing" than mine. I don't think we went to the same China.

January 25, 1999

Lauren and I have started waving wildly to the mailman and he waves very enthusiastically back. There were many good things in the mail today from some of the other families in our China travel group. We had a letter from Cathy and Henry with a couple of photos. Emma looks wonderful. Her eyes are bright. She's so much bigger. And we had a picture and a note from Dave and Theresa. Elizabeth is well too. Dave and Theresa also sent us a copy of the videotape they made in China: Wuzhou in living color again. I want all the babies to be happy and healthy. I guess I'm looking for the fairy tale ending.

January 27, 1999

Lauren wakes up foul and surly and bellows the whole time I'm changing and dressing her. Her face is all scrunched up like an apple doll. But if I sing, she goes quiet. She looks up at me and tilts her head to the side. I know she's listening and I feel like I'm Mick Jagger at Madison Square Garden. I think I need to get out more.

I made an obstacle course. (Okay, I put the middle section from the table in the hallway.) We ran it over and over and over this morning. Lauren has no trouble staying with activities. It was her idea to run around the loop. So we walked across the table middle, then ran through the living room and kitchen, came back down the hall and did it all again.

"We" means Lauren and me. Pat gave up after about half a dozen circuits. I kept going, but stopped counting loops after twenty-seven. I think I was in the same mental zone marathoners get to in the last couple of miles of a race.

January 28, 1999

Maybe I'm not as bad a mother as I generally think I am. I was in the waiting room at the doctor's office when a couple of teenagers came in with their baby. They were feeding her potato chips and Coke. And I heard the mother say the baby was hungry because she'd thrown her Fruit Loops into the tub.

I let my kid have two chocolates and I felt guilty. I offered her a french fry once. Once. And I felt guilty.

If the number one emotion of motherhood is overwhelming love for your child, number two has to be guilt that you will do the wrong thing and she'll become a serial killer.

January 30, 1999

Lauren had a nightmare again last night. I put her on my lap, wrapped in my arms, and she held on as though she thought I was going to disappear.

I kept her in our bed until she was sleepy. She didn't make another sound all night. I checked her four times. I put my face down by the bottom of the bars, so I could feel her breath on my cheek.

February 3, 1999

If Lauren gets kicked out of playschool someday, it will be Pat's fault. He taught her to say the word "poop." I have a kid who can say poop clearly, but insists on calling me Bubba. It's her best word next to bye-bye.

I wouldn't want to do this alone. I don't mean I think it's wrong or I couldn't. It's just that I like having someone who is as enthralled by everything Lauren does as I am. When she learned to pick up a Cheerio between her thumb and finger, instead of sliding it across her face to her mouth with the palm of her hand, I wanted to talk about it all day. Okay, I did talk about it all day. But so did Pat.

I think other people are starting to cross the street when they see me coming.

February 5, 1999

This morning I watched Pat unsnap Lauren's pant legs, whip off the diaper, clean her, get the new one snugly in place and the pants back on. "Getting pretty good at that, Dad," I said, as he set her on her feet and we watched her take off down the hall.

"I didn't think I'd ever get the hang of putting on a diaper," he said. "Or those goddamn sleepers, or any of it. I felt so incompetent when we first got home. I'd lay awake and listen at night in case she cried, and I didn't know what the hell I'd do if she did."

"But you're so good with her," I said.

"Yeah, because I know what I'm doing, at least some of the time," he said. "And she's used to me and I'm used to her. I didn't want to let her or you down. I decided I wasn't going to run away the way I used to."

I hugged him. "You're good at this. I swear," I said.

"I don't know if I am or not," he said. "But I can't imagine life without her."

Neither can I.

February 9, 1999

This child can hold a grudge. (I didn't teach her that.) Sunday afternoon she was on my lap at the table while I was making a list and I let her scribble with my pencil for a moment. When Pat came in, she ran out to see him with the pencil in her hand. He took it away, because she shouldn't be running with a pencil.

Lauren was enraged. She yelled. She stomped her feet. She shook her little arms. I went downstairs to get a couple of crayons and I could hear it all thumping over my head, like a kick-line of elephants. As soon as I handed over the crayons, the tantrum was over, but she froze out Pat. When he leaned over for a kiss, she slid away from him on my lap and he didn't even get a glance. She didn't stay mad at him for long, but while she was angry she was single-minded about it. I know, I'm not supposed to think this is a good thing, but it is funny to me how strong-willed she can be.

Yesterday we tried no morning nap. Bob and Rhonda came over and Lauren was wired from showing off. She wouldn't sleep in the afternoon either. She fired Bill, Dolly and both blankets out of the crib. She almost got the fitted sheet off the mattress by bracing her feet on the railing at one corner and yanking at it with both hands.

At four this morning, she was crying. My brain clicks on right away, but my body doesn't, so I'm stumbling and running into the door and the walls and I never remember to grab my robe. As soon as I picked her up, she put her cheek against mine and stopped crying.

I've been waiting for this for a long time. I wrapped her in a blanket and we sat in the rocking chair for a while. I wish I could fix everything that makes her cry for the rest of her life so easily.

February 14, 1999

Only seventeen months old and she's smitten with her first guy. And of course he's an older man. He's five.

Roger Miller came to visit with his grandson Mackenzie. He used to work with Pat. Lauren got that adoring look on her face and kept putting a hand on Mac's blonde hair. He's the first person close to her size whom she's been around since China. All she wanted to do was stand close to Mac, laugh and touch his hair. I can see she's not going to be the type to play hard to get.

Everything is going by so quickly. Yesterday Lauren walked up to the bedroom door, made a little fist and knocked. How did she learn to do that? She's discovered that if she blows into the open end of one of her giant pop-beads it makes a whistling sound. We've been having impromptu concerts all day.

She brushes her hands off when she has something on her fingers, just the way I do. She tries to pull her hands back through her hair. And she'll stick out her lower lip sometimes and exhale the way I do when I'm frustrated. I can see bits of myself in her. Sometimes it makes me laugh and sometimes it scares me.

February 16, 1999

We went to get our last hepatitis booster shots today at the travel clinic. Lauren smiled and did that you-may-kiss-my-hand thing she's currently doing with strangers.

Lauren may be getting spoiled from being the center of attention, but I know I'm getting way too much fun out of showing her off. Every time someone tells me how cute she is, I'm half expecting a roll of thunder or a lightning flash just above my head as a reminder that I actually had nothing to do with it.

People have children for all sorts of reasons. Or for no reason. They have them by design or because there was nothing on television or because the backseat of the car really is more comfortable.

I wanted a child; that's my reason for adopting Lauren. I've had my moments of feeling very self-righteous and then the little voice in the back of my head whispers, selfish, selfish. What makes my reason better than anyone else's?

February 18, 1999

I lie in bed sometimes and create stories for myself about the three months Lauren may have spent with her birth mother. Was her other mother married, single, a student, a farm worker, educated, poor? I know Lauren is strong and resilient with a bit of a rebellious streak. Someone gave those qualities to my baby.

In the morning as soon as Lauren's dressed she races over to the night-light and points at it until I turn it off. The day can't start until that's done. She has this strong sense of how things are supposed to be. I think it probably comes from being almost one-and-a-half.

And maybe a little of it comes from living with me.

March 3, 1999

The six-month assessment papers arrived from Children's Bridge today. Eight pages of questions about Lauren's health, her development and how she is adjusting to her new home. This is the last formality we have to deal with. The paperwork will be sent back to China so that their adoption officials can be assured Lauren is being well taken care of, and that she's settled with us. I am so tired of filling out forms. Is "none of your business" considered a satisfactory answer?

March 5, 1999

We took Lauren to George's today for a pair of shoes. Louie George found a little pair of tan boots that look like little work boots. How am I supposed to know if they fit? We walked all around the store — on the carpet and the floor — and I took Lauren's socks off to check her feet for rub or pinch marks. I don't know if I was supposed to do that, but it seemed like a good idea to me.

As soon as we were home, she grabbed my hand and we walked down the hall to admire how smashing she looked in her mirror. Then we walked back to the kitchen. And back to the mirror again. We did that same circuit for close to twenty minutes. Lauren was so excited with that big open-mouth grin she gets when she's really happy. I've never had this kind of experience with shoes. Either I'm frazzled because it took so long to find them, or crazy because they cost so much.

March 7, 1999

Lauren has two molars almost all the way up and I didn't know. We were making faces in the tub tonight and I thought I saw an extra tooth. I said,

"Open wide," and there they were: a molar on each side on the bottom.

I feel as though I'm brushing Tarzan's teeth twice a day. When I say, "Open wide," first she lets out this bellow. Then we brush.

I am so lucky that she's so easy about everything. I could pretty much do everything wrong and I think she'd still be okay.

March 10, 1999

Now Lauren has started taking out the round roasting pan, getting up on top of it, and dancing. We clap. Then she extends her hand for someone to help her down and I say, "Take a bow." And she dips from the waist until her head almost touches the floor.

She even takes the show on the road. She just picks up the roaster as the spirit moves her and we've had dancing in the bathroom, the hallway and the living room.

March 11, 1999

Lauren is seventeen-and-a-half pounds now and over twenty-nine inches tall. She isn't a baby anymore. I walk into her room and she looks up and smiles at me, and it's like every light in the world came on all at the same time.

We'd been folding towels downstairs this afternoon and when I reached down to pick up Lauren she took my hand instead and climbed onto the bottom step. Then she lifted her foot, put it on the next tread and looked up at me. "Go for it," I said. She went to the next step and the next, all the way to the top. I swung her into my arms and said, "You are a genius baby." When I set her down she walked around with her chin jutting out, looking very proud.

After supper as soon as we were downstairs she was ready to climb, with a glint in her eye that makes me think we're going to have to keep her away from motorcycles and parachutes when she's older. And young men who have either one. At the top of the stairs, I showed her how to slide down from tread to tread on her backside.

I can see that my secret fear that she would be sixteen and still wouldn't know how to climb stairs isn't going to happen.

April 4, 1999

We left Lauren with Mum for the first time today. We went for a walk and we were probably out of the house for about half an hour. I know she needs to get used to both of us being gone. And I need to get better at leaving her. I kept sneaking looks back over my shoulder even when I couldn't see the house any longer, and trying to make Pat walk faster. He patted my arm once and said, "She's fine." And I knew he was right.

But the world seems to be full of land mines now. And monsters and evil and things I never noticed before. So far we haven't seen any prejudice. This is a university town with lots of foreign students and there's tolerance, if not always respect.

We've had Lauren now for six months. Everyone says the time goes by so fast and it does but you don't understand that until you're experiencing it yourself. I still feel on edge most of the time, but God or someone seems to have turned the volume down to a level I can live with.

April 6, 1999

I took Lauren to Gwen, my stylist, for her first haircut — by someone who knows what she's doing — a short little bob with bangs. Lauren sat on the booster seat and watched with great seriousness in the mirror.

We went back for Lauren's follow-up blood tests this morning. She cried and grabbed me so tightly I could feel her fingernails dig into my arm. For a moment, I could see myself swinging my purse at the lab technicians and running for the parking lot.

April 8, 1999

She had her first lollipop today. Pat sat on the kitchen floor holding onto it and she kept coming and giving it a lick.

Lick.

Run into the living room and back.

Lick.

Pull the pots out of the cupboard.

Lick.

Play drum solo.

Lick.

Dance and take a bow.

Lick.

I blew Lauren a kiss the way I've done probably a thousand times before and today she blew one back and about six more. I always kiss my palm and hold it out and she did the same — even the smacking sound. Just when I think it's not possible to love her more, she sneaks up on me with something like this.

April 13, 1999

In the mall this afternoon, we met a teenager with her baby. He was just nine months old and so beautiful with wispy white-blond hair and blue eyes.

His mother was probably about sixteen. She looked tired. Her shiny lipstick was half chewed off and her nails were bitten down to nubs. I watched how carefully she picked the baby up from his stroller. She rubbed his cheek with a finger and smiled at him.

We walked over and Lauren reached out her hand. The baby grabbed a finger and she smiled at him. He grinned back. His mother and I made the kind of small talk I make all the time now with women I don't know. "How old is he?" "How long has she been walking?" "Is he sleeping through the night?"

Meanwhile Lauren and the baby babbled in their secret baby code, probably plotting a little baby uprising. I pictured little placards with, "No more naps" and "Down with strained peas."

Being a mother is so much easier for me than for that teenage mother. I'm not sixteen and trying to figure out who I am and what I want my life to be. Good or bad, much of that work's been done. I have patience (some), experience, time and money. I've already done a lot of the things I wanted to do. And I have someone with whom to share Lauren, who loves her just as much as I do.

April 17, 1999

Twice now I've caught myself using the word "born" instead of "adopted" when I'm talking about Lauren. Then I have to correct myself. I did go all the way to China and it's not as though I actually think I pushed that watermelon head of hers through my loins. It just doesn't seem that relevant on a day-to-day basis.

Time has definitely sped up since Lauren arrived. I know I have the same seven days in a week that I had before, but they seem to be going by twice as fast, as though I'd hit my fast-forward button. I keep trying to find the pause so I can get my breath and fix all the good parts in my memory, but life just keeps zipping on by at double speed.

Every day Lauren is becoming more independent. I try to picture who we'll both be in the future.

I left her for a whole morning with Pat while I went to the store for applesauce and diapers, and then for a haircut and ten minutes alone in the library. I lifted her into a hug and she wiggled away, chanting, "Up-pah, up-pah," which means both up and down. She stood on the wide ledge of the living room window, her father holding on behind her, as I drove away and sent me an offhand wave. The bus was rolling by the end of the court. Across the street in Mrs. Munro's yard a calico cat was stalking robins. The world is full of an infinite number of things more interesting than Mommy leaving.

The baby I first held is gone. Already I'm getting glimpses of who Lauren is going to be. I hope she has a long and wonderful life. I hope I'm around to see most of it. I hope I'm a long way from waist-high underpants and strained prunes. But I know that when I get there it's going to feel as though I just blinked between there and here.

EPILOGUE

We've come so far from that moment I first lifted Lauren into my arms and fell in love in the space between one second and the next. That small, wobbly baby with the big bald spot on the back of her head is a pig-tailed four-year-old who shimmies up the door-frame to turn on the light.

From the first time I held her I was certain Lauren was meant to be my child. But I wasn't prepared for the depth of her need for me or of mine for her. She sends the full force of her love at me and I'm never quite sure whether I'm living up to it. But I can't imagine living without it.

She likes to touch my leg or my arm as I go past her playing in a patch of sunlight on the living room floor. She wanders by to tickle me while I'm making the bed, and presses her cheek to my face for a moment while we cook supper. We watch *Arthur* together on TV and she leans her body into mine, one arm draped across my back.

I like to watch Lauren sleep. It's the only time she's ever quiet. While she's awake there are stories to share, songs to sing and questions about everything. Why? What? Where?

She is good-natured, but strong willed and intense. Sometimes she disobeys with defiance shining in her eyes and then before I can say anything puts herself in the corner. She's quick to hug, to smile, to climb in my lap, to slide her arms around my neck and whisper, "I love you," in my ear. I still can't think of a better sound than her laughter.

I think about Lauren's birth mother sometimes. Is that where Lauren's long feet with their beautiful high arches come from? Was it from her birth mother that she got her talent for music? Who gave my child her unnerving ability to scamper to the top of the monkey bars?

Each night she plants a kiss on the large map of China in her room. "You tell me story 'bout China," she says. And I tell her about the night I first saw her, or about the bus ride to Wuzhou. When she's older we want to go back to China. I hope the trip will answer some of the questions I expect she'll have by then.

Like most other four-year-olds, Lauren is torn between being independent and being my baby. She loves sourdough bagels, Chinese cabbage, ginger ale and noodles. She adores the Dixie Chicks and Bryan Adams. She's already mastered chopsticks, pulling them impatiently from her father's hands, insisting, "Let me do it!"

She drags me to the long mirror on her bedroom door and holds up her arms. I swing her up into mine and she calls, "Daddy, come here." When he does her arms go around both of us and she grins and says, "We a family." And we are.

"What would have happened to her, if you hadn't adopted her?" more than one well-meaning person has asked. That's something I never think about. I know someone else would have adopted Lauren. But sometimes, I wonder what would have happened to me. I wonder if I would have become somebody self-absorbed, cynical and afraid of life.

There are so many places during the adoption process where things could have gone differently and sent us in a different direction. And this enchanting, funny, resilient, stubborn, curious, loving child would not be mine. But they didn't. And she is. A miracle. Miracles, I've learned, happen after months of waiting, endless questions and stacks of paperwork. But they do happen.

SUGGESTED RESOURCES

BOOKS

Bascom, Barbara B. and Carole A. McKelvey. *The Complete Guide to Foreign Adoption.* New York: Pocket Books, 1997.

Buck, Pearl S. *The Good Earth.* New York: Washington Square, 1994.

Dann, Patty. *Baby Boat: A Memoir of Adoption.* New York: Hyperion, 1998.

Evans, Karin. *The Lost Daughters of China.* New York: Tarcher, 2000.

Katz, Karen. *Over the Moon: An Adoption Tale.* New York: Henry Holt, 1997.

Lindsay, Jeanne. *Pregnant? Adoption is an Option.* Buena Park: Morning Glory, 1997.

McColm, Michelle. *Adoption Reunions.* Toronto: Second Story, 1993.

McCutcheon, John. *Happy Adoption Day.* Toronto: Little Brown, 1996.

Reynolds, Nancy. *Adopting Your Child.* North Vancouver: Self-Counsel, 1993.

Schaefer, Carol. *The Other Mother: A Woman's Love for the Child She Gave Up for Adoption.* New York: Soho, 1991.

Tan, Amy. *The Joy Luck Club.* New York: Putnam, 1989.

Thomas, Eliza. *The Road Home.* New York: Dell, 1997.

Wadia-Ells, Susan. *The Adoption Reader: Birth Mothers, Adoptive Mothers & Adopted Daughters Tell Their Stories.* Toronto: Seal, 1995.

Waldron, Jan L. *Giving Away Simone: A True Story of Daughters, Mothers, Adoption & Reunion.* Toronto: Random House, 1995.

Wine, Judith. *The Canadian Adoption Guide: A Family at Last.* Toronto: McGraw-Hill Ryerson, 1995.

Zhang, Song Nan. *The Children of China: An Artist's Journey.* Toronto: Tundra, 1999.

WEB SITES

www.adoption.ca
Adoption Council of Canada

www.adoptivefamiliesmagazine.com

www.calib.com/naic
National Adoption Information Clearinghouse
Extensive source of information for Americans on both domestic and international adoption.

www.childrensbridge.com
The Children's Bridge
1400 Clyde Ave., Suite 221
Nepean, ON K2G 3J2

www.china-ccaa.org
China Centre for Adoption Affairs

www.cic.gc.ca
Citizenship and Immigration Canada

www.familyhelper.net
Adoption information for both Canadians and Americans.
For information about their newsletter write to:
Adoption Helper
Box 1353
Southampton, ON N0H 2L0

www.fwcc.org
Families with Children from China

www.iccadopt.org
International Concerns for Children Inc.
Produces the *Report on Intercountry Adoption* and a quarterly newsletter.
ICC
911 Cypress Drive
Boulder, CO 80303-2821

www.ins.usdoj.gov
Immigration and Naturalization Service

www.jcics.org
Joint Council on International Children's Services
1320 Nineteenth Street N.W., Suite 200
Washington, DC 20036

www.nacac.org
North American Council on Adoptable Children
Offers a quarterly newsletter for all NACAC members.
NACAC
970 Raymond Ave., Suite 106
St. Paul, MN 55114

www.raisingadoptedchildren.com
Publishes the *Adopted Child* newsletter.

www.toddlersonline.com/adopt
More information on adoption for Canadians

http://travel.state.gov/int'ladoption.html
Extensive information about international adoption from The Office of Children's
Issues, US State Dept.
Office of Children's Issues
2401 E Street, N.W., Room L127
Washington, D.C. 20037